INTO THE CLASSROOM:
The Outward Bound® Approach to Teaching and Learning

by
Mitchell Sakofs
and George P. Armstrong

with
Tom James
Scott Hartl
Denis Udall
Jon Howard

 KENDALL/HUNT PUBLISHING COMPANY
4050 Westmark Drive   Dubuque, Iowa 52002

CREDITS
Photos: Copyright © Walter Silver
Page 151, "In Hardwood Groves". From THE POETRY OF ROBERT FROST edited by
Edward Connery Lathem. Copyright © 1962 by Robert Frost. Copyright 1934 © 1969
by Henry Holt and Co., Inc. Reprinted by permission of Henry Holt and Co., Inc.

National Headquarters
Route 9D
R2 Box 280
Garrison, NY 10524-9757

(914) 424-4000

ISBN 0-7872-1972-X

Printed in the United States of America
10 9 8 7 6 5 4 3 2 1

ACKNOWLEDGMENT

What started as a small group discussion among staff representing all the Outward Bound® schools and centers has become a reality. The intent of this book was to pull together the philosophical concepts and some of the activities practiced on Outward Bound courses, and to present them in a form that could be easily used by classroom teachers. With the creative and innovative help and input of many people in and around Outward Bound, we have done that.

This book would not be possible without the authorship of specific chapters, material submissions and editorial help from Greg Farrell, Gerry Golins, Tom James, Arnold Shore, Scott Hartl, Tina Clark, Dennis Udall, Jon Mark Howard, Bill Quinn, Jasper Hunt, and many other Outward Bound instructors, course directors, program directors, school directors and friends. Special thanks to Ted Rodman, 501c3 Group, for book design, photography direction and prepress production and to Walter Silver for photography.

The authors are very grateful to all the contributors and to the people in Outward Bound that helped make this book possible. A special thanks to the DeWitt Wallace Reader's Digest Fund and the Dragon Foundation for their assistance and support.

The contributors to the activities and lesson sections are:

Phil Costello	Steven J. Rippe
Charles Reade	Kim Marshall
Gruffie Clough	Susan Lincoln
Jake Jagel	Lewis Glenn
Peter Bailey	Rick Gordon
Kelly Gregg	Sterling Catkey
Huck Truitt	Deb Eads
John Dutton	Susan McCray
Debra C. Banks	Jim Austin
Flo Levin	Jerry Townsend
Nanci Ohnesorge	Helen Fouhey
Chris Carrigan	Trina Abbott

PREFACE

Welcome to Outward Bound® and active learning.

This book is about bringing joy and adventure to teaching and learning.

The fundamental tenets of this book are the beliefs that:

1. All people can and want to learn.

2 . Learning and understanding take place when people engage in and reflect upon challenging experiences in which they must make choices, take responsible action, acquire new skills, and work together.

3. Personal experience and intellectual growth are drawn together through adventure and challenge to help students build an understanding of themselves and the world around them.

4 . With care, compassion and respect for different learning styles and backgrounds, teachers play a vital role in guiding students along this journey.

5. Outward Bound can help teachers unlock students' passions for learning, and thus build within them the skills, knowledge, courage, fitness and perseverance to imagine and work toward realizing a better world.

In this book you will find activities and lessons you can use with your students to build community, cultivate compassion and moral conviction, nurture leadership, teach academics and equip them with the skills to be lifelong learners. You will also find an explanation of Outward Bound's philosophy as well as the basic components and educational principles of Outward Bound's most recent initiative in public education — Expeditionary Learning.

The activities, curricula, perspectives and ideas presented in this book were developed by teachers who are themselves exploring the application of Outward Bound's educational ideas and practices to the business of teaching in schools. Their writings represent a quest for knowledge, and we present them with the hope that you will take from this book not only perspectives, activities, curricula and ideas, but the inspiration to bring them into your everyday work.

This book is a starting point.

Mitchell Sakofs
George P. Armstrong

CONTENTS

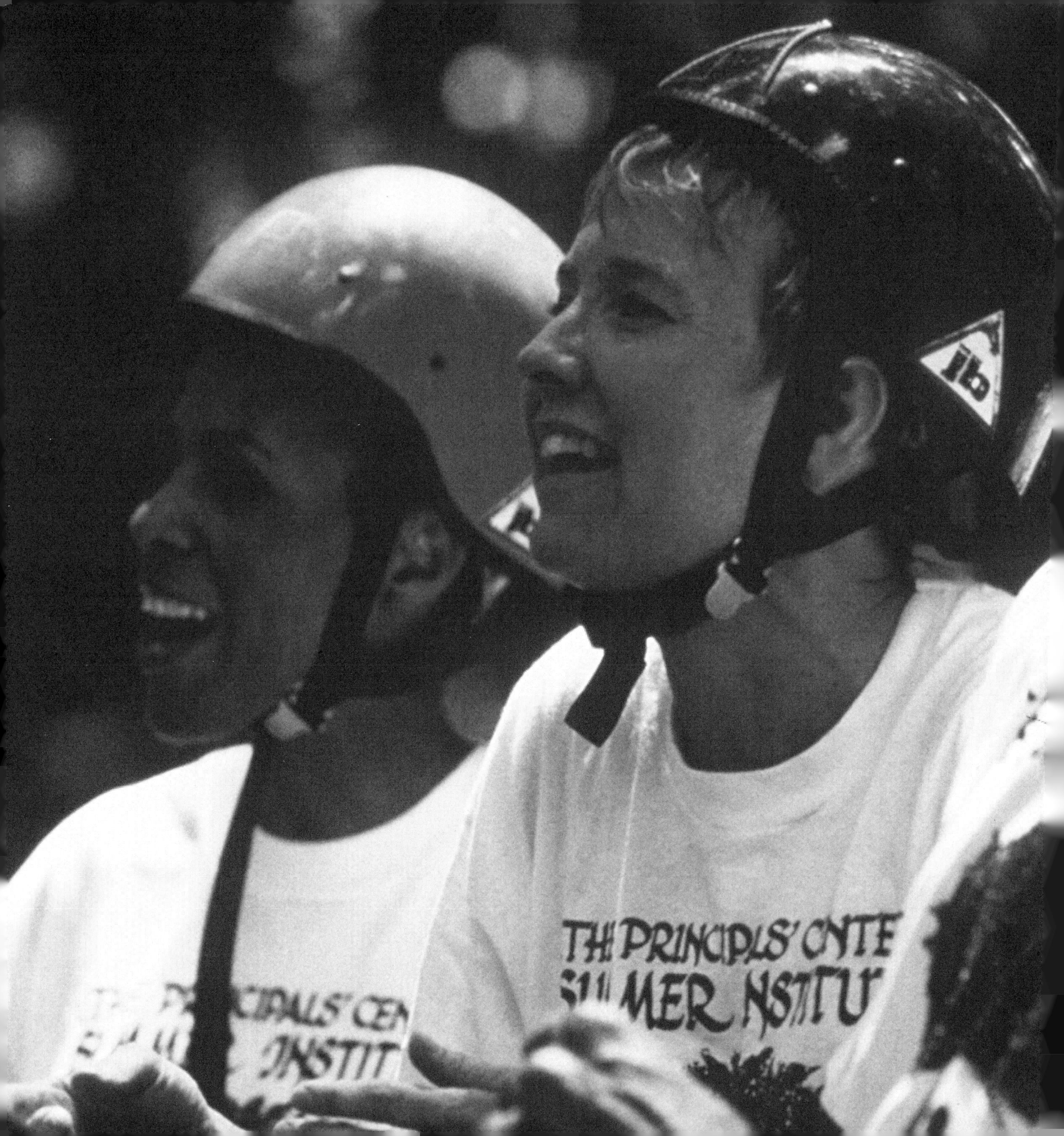
PRINCIPALS'

FOREWORD

There is a revolution sweeping public education today and the key to its success lies with teachers on the front line. But the outcome of this revolution is by no means guaranteed. Current proponents of change know what they are railing against, but are not quite sure what to put in its place. This lack of vision will kill the fire just as quickly as that clump of snow did in the Jack London classic, *To Build a Fire*.

This book, *Into The Classroom: The Outward Bound Approach To Teaching and Learning,* is written to help teachers formulate a productive vision for the kind of teaching-learning situation where participation and enthusiasm are high, and where indications abound that significant learning takes place.

The experience of all of the book's contributors with Outward Bound runs deep. I started, for instance, as an instructor with the Colorado Outward Bound School and eventually became its school director. In addition, we all have demonstrated an abiding interest in traditional schooling. My first assignment was teaching sixth grade to the children of migratory farm workers.

While we offer this vision with conviction, it should not be taken as gospel. Each teacher has the responsibility of developing his or her unique approach. Hopefully this book will be a useful resource in doing just that.

In developing my own model for teaching and learning, I start by asking a fundamental question: What set of conditions or circumstances make people use their resources to the fullest? The fact that people excel as small group problem solvers revealed itself to me after years of watching participants tackle so-called "initiatives" in Outward Bound. Take a classic initiative like "The Wall," the object of which is to get everyone over an eleven foot high wall without anyone being able to go back down to help. Time after time, ordinary groups of people presented with The Wall would do extraordinary things, much as if their very lives depended on it and they had known each other for years. Without hesitation they would sacrifice vanity, pride, ego and clothes to accomplish their objective. It was as if something primordial clicked and they went into overdrive. They became totally engrossed in the here and now, applying whatever they had learned in life to solve the riddle. Just how do you get the last person up? Inevitably they would find a solution. There was no denying the genuine satisfaction they derived from their achievements, nor the learning that took place.

If you see people as problem solvers, then one purpose of education is to develop their problem-solving skills. Since experience is invariably the best teacher, the teacher's job essentially is to pose problems which require educational experiences to resolve. Such an idea creates demands that are much different from those of traditional teaching.

Photo Left: **Participants in Thompson Island Outward Bound's "Connecting With Courage" women's program experience the rewards of teamwork and support.**

In the problem-solving model we accumulate knowledge not just by retaining and regurgitating it, but by applying it to solve problems. Know-how becomes more important than knowledge, and takes re-focusing on developing critical thinking skills. Critical thinking is required in problem solving: you're required to use pertinent knowledge, analyze the situation, hypothesize a solution, implement the decision, evaluate the results, and learn from the experience.

The problem-solving approach is dynamic. Unlike the traditional approach, which sees the student as an empty vessel to be filled with facts and figures, problem-solving begins with a concept of the student as resourceful and capable of exercising common sense and self-determination. These assumptions should translate into heightened expectations for achievement.

To have a fair assurance of success, the problems posed must tie in with what the student knows or can know. The teacher must respect the learner's needs for security and his inherent fear of the unknown. Yet the problems must be challenging. Safety is important, but so is risk taking. Challenging the learner introduces anxiety into the equation, and anxiety is a spark igniting the learning process. In the classic "fight or flight" situation, there are really three avenues available to the learner. He either opts out or drops out, muddles through, or has an exalted, exuberant response.

The trick to ensuring that the learner either copes or thrives, both of which are positive, is to pose a problem in which the resolution has consequence to the student. There must be something to be gained or lost by challenging oneself. In short, there must be meaning.

Once with a patrol of Outward Bound students, we were camped in preparation to climb the famed S Ridge of Snowmass Mountain in Colorado. The ridge towered above us like a monolithic serpentine. As I pitched my tarp, I noticed one of my students, a young woman, sitting away from her mates, facing the ridge, all hunched over. I quietly walked over and sat down beside her, saying nothing for awhile. Finally, I said, "I bet you're having a hard time seeing yourself climbing that ridge." With that she burst into tears. After she confirmed my suspicions, I asked her, "Is there a pattern here? Are there other things you opt out of beforehand because you can't see yourself succeeding?" It turned out there were. In fact, she told me, she had an opportunity to go to nursing school, but she was afraid of turning in her application for fear of not being accepted. "Well then," I said, "this mountain is your opportunity to change that pattern once and for all." I suggested she climb right behind me, which she did to start off, and that she concentrate on climbing one step at a time. Well, she climbed it, conquering her fears. The experience had a lasting effect. Later that fall I got a letter from her telling me that she had applied to nursing school, been accepted, and was doing well. Before our conversation she was consumed by fear. There had been nothing to be gained by sticking out her neck. When she gained perspective, taking the risk became worthwhile. Snowmass became "the mountain worth climbing." It became her metaphor for success.

Meaningful challenges are available in academic disciplines, but they are not as easy to come by as they are in Outward Bound. Outward Bound problems have "sizzle" (high risk/high reward). In a sense they offer a hero quest, where mastery is worthy of acclaim. For the most part students are there because they want to be. It is easy to concentrate and learn because the students are isolated in an evocative setting and given sufficient time to learn a few things well. While the course is intense, its duration is relatively short; there is light at the end of the tunnel. It is easier to marshall one's resources when there is a clearly defined end in sight.

Enter the real world—your world. Attendance is mandatory, with much passive (and active) resistance to overcome. There are many distractions and overriding everyday concerns undermining the learning process. Custodial duties and irrelevant curriculum mandates limit your freedom to innovate. Comprehensive subject matter is presented piecemeal in segmented forty-minute periods over a protracted period of time. It is hard to learn anything when you cannot sink your teeth into it. Such conditions are trying; but they are not insurmountable.

It helps to structure the curriculum thematically and offer a wide range of things to investigate. The wider the range, the likelier there will be something to interest everyone. Offer as many opportunities for choice as possible. Choice is the elixir of learning. It fosters responsibility and accountability as the learner becomes a stakeholder. Draw the problems from the real world, increasing the chance of relevancy. Whenever possible locate implementation in the real world outside the school grounds. If, for example, you are studying the criminal justice system, you might hold mock trials in real courtrooms. Choose themes ripe with unresolved issues; they foster creativity, and enhance the motivation to learn. The will to create is linked to the possibility of controlling one's own destiny. The ability to shape one's future is really the benefit of having "the big brain." The more a teacher denies creativity, the more he or she squelches the learner's spirit.

Allow for concentration. We know there is little opportunity for success without focus. If you are working in a tightly structured school environment, one thing you can do to increase concentration is to reduce the breadth of what is covered while increasing the depth. In the problem-solving paradigm quality is more important than quantity; effectiveness more important than efficiency.

It helps to be flexible with the use of time. Revelations, insights and breakthroughs often occur when fatigue has set in, the defenses are down, and the parties involved are ready to see the light. It is rare that such a state can be reached during a regular classroom schedule. Of course you can't go "all out" all the time. Time must be taken to recharge your batteries. But you and your students should be able to turn on the "afterburners" when needed. Ironically, extracurricular activities enjoy this kind of flexibility. The precedent is there.

Engage all the faculties of the learner simultaneously. I remember an astronaut remarking that captaining a paddle raft through some of the major rapids on the Green River was the closest he had come to space flight. At first I was astonished that white-water river running could be put on

Revelations, insights and breakthroughs often occur when fatigue has set in, the defenses are down, and the parties involved are ready to see the light.

a par with space flight. Then I got the picture. When he was captaining the raft through the rapids, he was not thinking about captaining the raft, he was totally absorbed in the task. Thinking, feeling, and being were in alignment. There was no room for detachment, for reservation, or even for objectivity. It was a sort of enlightenment.

The more the teacher can include "the head, the heart, and the hands" in learning, the more success there will be. When you segment the responses, it is like asking someone to compete with one hand tied behind his back. Holistic engagement invites the learner literally "to give it his all." Every learner has different strengths to draw on. Some are more physical, some analytical, some more perceptive. Others are more passionate or more nurturing. Holistic learning allows the learner to play to his or her strengths while developing those faculties in which he or she is not so strong. As a result, there are more opportunities for achievement and growth.

To elicit holistic responses, accomplish or produce something tangible. If you are studying physics, build and fire a rocket. If you are studying economics, start a business. The production of goods or services by students offers the possibility of presenting academic disciplines combined much as they are in real life.

Use your imagination; there are always holistic problem-solving opportunities available. I remember once doing a unit on war as a part of a western civilization course. I wanted students to experience military values, such as following orders and esprit de corps. I organized the class into drill teams. I tried to balance the teams with equal numbers of "hawks" and "doves." As in the military, leaders were arbitrarily chosen and individual achievement was dependent on group performance. Competition between groups was introduced to further develop esprit de corps. Soon groups were marching throughout the school grounds barking orders, counting cadence. Some students rebelled against the coercion; others revelled in it. Discussions got heated. Tempers flared. Where there is heat, there is the potential for light.

People need security, creativity, and competence, and they need to belong, to take part in a community, to contribute to something larger than themselves. The organization of your class into learning teams goes a long way to fulfilling social needs. Teams have unique properties that invite participation and dramatically increase the likelihood of success. A team is a special kind of group. It is the primary operating unit and probably the most functional one. Everyone's contribution in a team counts. No one can slack off without hurting the team's success. Five to twelve people is usually best.

The object is to maximize strengths and minimize weaknesses. If coached properly, the weaker members of the team are buoyed by the stronger; the less experienced by the more experienced. Leadership and followership are inevitable requirements. Students coach and teach each other, because the success of each individual is bound up with the success of the team. They practice and test democracy as the team struggles to work toward the common good. They must communicate.

The teacher must design, present and implement group problem-solving exercises. In the process, the teacher must be a facilitator of productive communication. I am talking about sharing thoughts and feelings, encouraging others to reciprocate and build consensus, resolve disagreements,

---

The more the teacher can include "the head, the heart, and the hands" in learning, the more success there will be.

confront values, brainstorm solutions, and discover meaning. The best way to teach these skills is to model them.

The teacher is now a manager, pointing groups in the right direction, listening in, relying whenever possible on the leadership in each group to keep it on track, intervening only when necessary. The group problem solving paradigm indisputably takes a lot more energy. If done right you should wear out your shoe soles going from one group to another.

There is a lot going on when a team tackles such learning opportunities. You must evaluate the solutions as well as the means employed to reach them. Can you adequately cover three groups of 10? It depends on the maturity of the students and the inherent risks in the situation. In the typical Outward Bound course, you could not.

How do we provide for more coverage in an austere budgetary environment? I think the greatest reservoir of relatively untapped, inexpensive talent is found in other students. An excellent example of this is the President's Leadership Class (PLC) at the University of Colorado. The PLC takes some of the most talented incoming freshmen and for two years offers them a variety of experiences to develop leadership skills. Each class is organized into teams managed by an upper-class PLC graduate. These upper-class proctors in turn are supervised by a professor. In exchange for their labor they are paid a small amount of money and provided with a wealth of experience in leadership. Senior citizens are another untapped and inexpensive source of talent. Quite often it is not money they are after, but involvement. Parent and community volunteers can be helpful, too, particularly if you tap into their areas of expertise and ask them for something specific.

There are other potential pitfalls. The unconventional schedule that typically accompanies such exercises can be stressful. Your leadership will be challenged. The problem-solving paradigm places as much emphasis on examining the means as the result. You must set the tone and help the team establish the ethical and moral parameters within which decision making should occur. Above all, your actions must be congruent with what you say. Your relationship with your colleagues will be challenged. Expect the old-timers to gripe, claiming that you are not covering the subject matter. And they will be right—you will not be covering the subject, you will be immersing students in it. You will be trading breadth for depth.

Fortunately the benefits outweigh the costs. You'll have the joy of watching enthusiastic learners and the satisfaction that comes from tapping more fully your own talents, and from having more meaningful relationships with students.

Can I promise you a rose garden? Hardly! Fundamental change is never pain free. Whether you start small or start big, by all means, just do it! To quote cowboy poetry, "there will be blood on the leather and tears in the eyes... swear at the Devil, then go for a ride."

Gerald L. Golins
Former director of the Colorado Outward Bound School
and current personnel director, Uintah County, CO

The teacher is now a manager, pointing groups in the right direction, listening in, relying whenever possible on the leadership in each group to keep it on track, intervening only when necessary.

HISTORICAL AND PHILOSOPHICAL PERSPECTIVES

Most people think of Outward Bound as high-adventure activities like rock climbing, mountaineering, white-water rafting, canoeing and camping. They associate it with pristine wilderness settings, grand vistas of snow-covered mountains, or serene back-country ponds lined by fir or spruce trees. They have images of teams of people crossing a rope bridge suspended high among the tree tops, or trying to climb a 12-foot high wooden wall equipped with nothing but their ingenuity.

Are these images accurate? Do they describe Outward Bound? Yes and no.

Yes, because programs offered through Outward Bound USA's seven schools and centers in Colorado, Maine, Massachusetts, North Carolina, Minnesota, New York and Oregon do conduct classes in some of the most beautiful and dramatic back-country environments in the world. Yes, because the physical and psychological challenges of back-country travel linked to group and individual initiative serve as a springboard for learning and emotional growth. But No, because they fail to illustrate Outward Bound's deep roots in education. No, because they do not represent the full spectrum of Outward Bound programs. They don't show the urban programs or the essential role of service in all our programs. And, they don't show Outward Bound's school-based programs that unfold in the classroom.

Photo Left: Kurt Hahn, the moving spirit of Outward Bound, employed challenge and outdoor adventure, not for their own sake, but as a way of teaching perseverance, skill, teamwork, leadership and compassionate service.

CHAPTER 1

The Only Mountain Worth Climbing:
The Search for Roots

> *I regard it as the foremost task of education to ensure survival of these qualities: an enterprising curiosity; an undefeatable spirit, tenacity in pursuit, readiness for sensible self-denial and above all, compassion.*
>
> — Kurt Hahn

Outward Bound is more than a set of methods and activities. It represents a core of values, a philosophy of education. In this broader sense, as well as in its applications as a specific method of learning, Outward Bound has a deep, historical affinity with conventional schooling.

The historical background is useful to consider when trying to understand the power of Outward Bound for improving schooling processes today. Kurt Hahn, the moving spirit of Outward Bound, employed challenge and outdoor adventure not for their own sake, but as a way of teaching perseverance, skill, teamwork, leadership, and compassionate service to the students at Gordonstoun, the school he founded in Scotland in the 1930s. By providing equipment, training, and safety-watch patrols made up of privileged students from his school, Hahn was able to extend the program of outdoor activity to include other children from poor families living near Gordonstoun. He created a sense of moral community around demanding personal commitments to such things as fitness, craftsmanship, and service.

He later widened this program into more systematic proposals such as the County Badge Scheme, Outward Bound, and the Duke of Edinburgh Award. Hahn's inclusion of poor children along with the rich established a cardinal principle that became part of Outward Bound in later years: Bring together people from different social classes in common pursuits leading to self-discovery and service to others.

With the coming of World War II, Kurt Hahn became aware of the devastating toll that German submarines were taking on British ships in the North Sea. Building upon his experience as an educator who had used challenging outdoor activities requiring cooperation and craftsmanship along with academic learning, he and others devised a program of intensive training for British Seamen from initiatives he had been running at his school. The program became Outward Bound, which took its name from the nautical term for a ship leaving port on a sea journey.

Special thanks to Tom James Ph. D., Brown University, for writing this chapter.

Outward Bound developed into a separate organization during the war and eventually became a worldwide movement in its own right, resulting in several dozen schools all over the world. But it is significant that the program first took shape, pedagogically, as an educational innovation arising from a secondary school.

To understand the potential of Outward Bound for helping teachers and learners in schools, it is useful to look more closely at Hahn's educational values. Born in 1886, Hahn was the second of four sons in a Jewish family in Berlin. Schooled with conventional German rigor at the Wilhelms gymnasium, he graduated in 1904. That same year he experienced a sunstroke that left him with a recurring disability for the rest of his life. Hahn read classics at Oxford from 1904 to 1906, with the support of his father, Oskar Hahn, industrialist and anglophile. From 1906 to 1910 he studied at various German universities—without, however, completing any degree. Returning to England in 1910, he continued to study at Oxford, and convalesced during the summers at Moray in northeastern Scotland, until the beginning of the Great War in 1914 called him home to Germany. He never achieved a degree beyond his secondary schooling.

During the war, Hahn served as a reader for the German Foreign Office and then the Supreme Command, reviewing English-language newspapers to gauge popular opinion. Politically, he allied himself with the those inside the German government who were seeking a negotiated peace in Western Europe instead of protracted war. Perceived as a liberal within the political atmosphere of his day, Hahn advocated greater restraint in pursuing German war aims. He espoused a code of responsibility that would be equally binding in war and peace; he used his influence behind the scenes to remind those in power about conciliatory factions at work within the governments of enemy nations.

At the end of the war, Prince Max von Baden asked Hahn to become his personal secretary. An articulate and enterprising young man, Hahn helped Prince Max, Germany's last imperial chancellor, complete his memoirs, probably writing as much as editing. Whatever the form of their collaboration, the two men left a record of tough-minded idealism and political vigilance. When Prince Max returned to spend his last years at the ancestral castle of his family at Schloss Salem, by Lake Constance, he took Kurt Hahn with him and they discussed projects to renew the ethical traditions of German social life, traditions they believed were threatened not only by extremism on the right and left, but by incomprehension, moral failings, and lack of will in the middle. In 1920, with Prince Max as benefactor, Hahn opened Salem School in part of the castle.

Salem School, which still operates today, was influenced by the educational ideas of Plato, Cecil Reddie's Abbotsholme and other English schools, and the example of country schools started by German educators under the leadership of Hermann Lietz. Salem represented an attempt to create a healthy environment in which young people could learn habits of life that would protect them against what Hahn saw as the deteriorating values of modern life. He identified the worst declines as those in fitness, skill and care, self-discipline, initiative and enterprise, memory and imagination, and compassion.

Directing the school from 1920 until 1933, Hahn placed greater emphasis on non-competitive physical activities and democratic forms of social cooperation than was the case in conventional German schools. At the urging of Prince Max, he incorporated egalitarian aims into the design of

> Salem represented an attempt to create a healthy environment in which young people could learn habits of life that would protect them against what Hahn saw as the deteriorating values of modern life. He identified the worst declines as those in fitness, skill and care, self-discipline, initiative and enterprise, memory and imagination, and compassion.

the school; while Salem naturally attracted the children of the wealthy, it also made space for, and actively sought, less-privileged students. Emulating the Cistercian monks who had inhabited the castle for many centuries, the students and teachers at Salem School helped the surrounding communities with various forms of service, including a fire brigade.

The curriculum at Salem prepared young people for higher education, but not without laying the groundwork for a life of moral and civic virtue, the chief aims of the school. Among the unusual assumptions underlying all forms of instruction at Salem was Hahn's conviction that students should experience failure as well as success. They should learn to overcome negative inclinations within themselves and prevail against adversity.

He believed, moreover, that students should learn to discipline their own needs and desires for the good of the community. They should realize through their own experience the connection between self-discovery and service. He also insisted that true learning required periods of silence and solitude as well as directed activity. Each day the students took a silent walk to commune with nature and revitalize their powers of reflection.

To keep mental and physical growth in balance, Hahn developed the notion of a training plan for his students, each of whom committed himself to an individually designed, gradually more challenging regimen of physical exercise and personal hygiene. Unlike the physical education program of other schools, the aim of the training plan was simply to establish good living habits, not to produce high levels of performance in competitive games.

By his early thirties, the schoolmaster was controversial, a gadfly, a target because he was a moral leader far beyond the lives of his students and teachers. In 1923 an attempted assassination failed. The director of Salem—the school's name means "peace"—idolized few men in his lifetime, but one incident he often recounted was the confrontation between Max Weber, Germany's most distinguished social scientist, and an angry crowd of leftist demonstrators in 1918. Weber shouted that he had never crawled before kings and emperors in the past, and he was not going to crawl before any mob now.

Similarly, Kurt Hahn refused to back down from the moral aims that animated every aspect of education as far as he was concerned. In a nation frighteningly polarized by the right and left in political debate, Hahn forced educational issues into the larger discussion of how society should be organized, and what people must do to maintain human decency in a world of conflict. No idyllic schoolmaster's life awaited him.

When it finally came, in the early 1930s, the controversy that pushed Kurt Hahn out of Germany involved the right and not the left. As the Nazis rose to power, the director of Salem School became an outspoken opponent. In 1932 a group of fascist storm troopers kicked a leftist activist to death before the eyes of his mother. Adolph Hitler immediately praised the action of his followers. Kurt Hahn wrote to the alumni of Salem, telling them to choose between Salem and Hitler. A man who knew Hahn at the time called it "the bravest deed in cold blood that I have ever witnessed." When he became the chief of state in 1933, Hitler imprisoned Hahn. Fortunately for the embattled educator, he still had friends in Britain who remembered his idealism and his hopes for friendship between the two nations. Prime Minister Ramsay MacDonald

Hahn forced educational issues into the larger discussion of how society should be organized, and what people must do to maintain human decency in a world of conflict.

and others helped to arrange for Hahn's release and timely emigration to England in 1933.

Within a year of his arrival, Kurt Hahn had started Gordonstoun, an institution that would become one of Britain's most distinguished progressive schools and serve as a model for similar schools in other countries. In the following decades, Hahn's educational vision served as the moving spirit for new institutions and programs of worldwide renown: the Moray Badge and County Badge Schemes and their successor, the Duke of Edinburgh Awards; Outward Bound; the Trevelyan Scholarships; and the United World Colleges.

Reaching back into this pre-history of Outward Bound, we might well look for the origins of the idea in 1913 instead of 1941 when Outward Bound was founded. For in the summer of 1913, instead of vacationing, as he had hoped, with a friend in Scotland, and still recuperating from a lingering illness resulting from the sunstroke he had suffered a few years before, Kurt Hahn outlined his idea for a school based on principles set forth in *Plato's Republic*. Hahn was twenty-eight years old and had never run a school, nor even taught in one. The ideal school he imagined never came into being, but it exerted a profound influence on all his subsequent efforts as an educator and statesman: Salem School, in Germany, in 1920; Gordonstoun School, in Scotland, in 1934; Outward Bound in Wales, in 1941; and Atlantic College, in England, in 1962.

In English Progressive Schools, Robert Skidelsky analyzes Hahn's debt to Plato as follows:

> Plato was a political reformer who sought to recall the Athenians to the old civic virtues eroded, as he saw it, by democratic enthusiasm and soft living. His aim was to educate a class of leaders in a "healthy pasture" remote from the corrupting environment, whose task it would be to regenerate society. Hahn must have been haunted by similar visions of decay as, inspired by these ideas, he drew up a plan in 1913 for a school modeled on Platonic principles. The war that broke out a year later and ended in the collapse of Germany was to give them a new urgency: to convert what might have remained a purely academic speculation into an active campaign for social and political regeneration.

Outward Bound places unusual emphasis on physical challenge, not as an end in itself, but as an instrument for training the will to strive for mastery. There is also the insistent use of action, instead of states of mind, to describe the reality of the individual. Education is tied unequivocally to experience, to what one does and not so much to one's attitudes and opinions.

A thread running from Plato through Hahn and through Outward Bound is the responsibility of individuals to make their personal goals consonant with social necessity. Not only is the part subordinated to the whole, but the part cannot even understand its own identity, its relations and its responsibility, until it has grasped the nature of the whole. Having stood up to Hitler before being exiled from Nazi Germany in 1933, Hahn believed in individual freedom, but he believed that students should be impelled into experiences that would teach them the bonds of social life necessary to protect such freedom. He took from Plato the idea that a human being cannot achieve perfection without becoming part of a perfect society—that is, without creating social harmony to sustain the harmonious life of the individual.

This is the overall structure of the argument in the *Republic*, and it is also the most important lesson

Outward Bound places unusual emphasis on physical challenge, not as an end in itself, but as an instrument for training the will to strive for mastery.

A thread running from Plato through Hahn and through Outward Bound is the responsibility of individuals to make their personal goals consonant with social necessity.

of an Outward Bound course, the lesson without which personal development is of questionable value. In a small group away from the degenerate ways of the world, the individual student comes to grips with what must be done to create a just society. In attempting to construct such a challenge, Hahn placed compassion above all other values of Outward Bound because it among all emotions is capable of reconciling individual strength with collective need.

The prospect of wholeness, the possibility, at least, of human life becoming an equilibrium sustained by harmony and balance, is what makes this form of education even thinkable. Skidelsky again offers a lucid analysis of the source of Hahn's thinking:

> The second idea which Hahn assimilated was Plato's notion that the principle of perfection was harmony and balance. The perfection of the body, he held, depends upon a harmony of its elements. Virtue (the health of the soul) is the harmony or balance between the various faculties of the psyche: reason, the appetites, and spirit. Virtue in the state is the harmony between its functional elements: thinkers, soldiers, and artisans. The same principle can be extended indefinitely—to relations between men, relations between states, and so on.

This passage sheds some light on Hahn's interest in giving his students experiences that would complement their strengths and weaknesses. In his speeches he said he wanted to turn introverts inside out and extroverts outside in. He wanted the poor to help the rich break their "enervating sense of privilege" and the rich to help the poor in building a true "aristocracy of talent."

The schools he founded sent bookworms to the playing field and jocks to the reading room. He did not produce outstanding athletes, but his students exhibited consistently high levels of fitness, accomplishment and social spirit. He said he valued mastery in the sphere of one's weakness over performance in the sphere of one's strength.

Hahn was indebted to other thinkers as well: Rousseau, Goethe, and William James, to name a few. William James, for example, in his essay "The Moral Equivalent of War," asked if it is not possible in time of peace to build the kind of social spirit and productivity one takes for granted in time of war. Hahn saw Outward Bound as an answer to that question. Goethe wrote of an education that would need to occur in a place apart, a "Pedagogical Province," so that individuals could be strengthened and given skills to survive, individually and collectively, in the debilitating environment of human society as we know it. Hahn was indebted to Rousseau, both for the idea that awakening an individual's collective concern is the key to healthy personal development and also for Rousseau's assumption that nature is an educator in its own right, more akin to the true human being than the society humans have built for themselves.

Hahn remarked once that we are in the Western world confronted by a progressive inhumanity of the society in which we live. He said that he saw Outward Bound as a countervailing force against the decline of initiative, due, in his words, to the widespread disease of "spectatoritis," the decline of skill and care due to weakening traditions of craftsmanship, and the decline of concern about one's neighbor due to the unseemly haste with which daily life is conducted. In 1930, three years before his exile from Germany for opposing Hitler, he drew up "The Seven Laws of Salem" to describe his educational methods (see page 8).

The schools he founded sent bookworms to the playing field and jocks to the reading room. He did not produce outstanding athletes, but his students exhibited consistently high levels of fitness, accomplishment and social spirit. He said he valued mastery in the sphere of one's weakness over performance in the sphere of one's strength.

The Seven Laws of Salem

1. **Give the children opportunities for self-discovery.**
   Every boy and girl has a grande passion, often hidden and unrealized to the end of life. The educator cannot hope and may not try to find it out by psychoanalytical methods. It can and will be revealed by the child coming into close touch with a number of different activities. When a child has come "into his own," you will often hear a shout of joy, or be thrilled by some other manifestation of primitive happiness.

2. **Make the children meet with triumph and defeat.**
   It is possible to wait on a child's inclinations and gifts and to arrange carefully for an unbroken series of successes. You may make him happy in this way—I doubt it—but you certainly disqualify him for the battle of life. Salem believes you ought to discover the child's weakness as well as his strength. Allow him to engage in enterprises in which he is likely to fail, and do not hush up his failure. Teach him to overcome defeat.

3. **Give the children the opportunity of self-effacement in the common cause.**
   This applies even for the youngsters out to undertake tasks that are of definite importance for the community. Tell them from the start: "You are a crew, not passengers. Let the responsible boys and girls shoulder duties big enough, when negligently preformed, to wreck the State."

4. **Provide periods of silence.**
   Follow the great precedent of the Quakers. Unless the present day generation acquires early habits of quiet and reflection, it will be speedily and prematurely used up by the nerve-exhausting and distracting civilization of today.

5. **Train the imagination.**
   You must call it into action, otherwise it becomes atrophied like a muscle not in use. The power to resist the pressing stimulus of the hour and the moment cannot be acquired in later life; it often depends on the ability to visualize what you plan and hope and fear for the future. Self-indulgence is in many cases due to lack of vision.

6. **Make games (i.e., competition) important but not predominant.**
   Athletics do not suffer by being put in their place. In fact you restore the dignity of the usurper by dethroning him.

7. **Free the sons of the wealthy and powerful from the enervating sense of privilege.**
   Let them share the experiences of an enthralling school life with sons and daughters of those who have to struggle for their existence. No school can build up a tradition of self-discipline and vigorous but joyous endeavor unless at least 30 percent of the children come from homes where life is not only simple, but even hard.

Writing in 1941, Hahn listed the benefits that such an education offered the individual student: "He will have a trained heart and a trained nervous system which will stand him in good stead in fever, exposure and shock; he will have acquired spring and powers of acceleration; he will have built up stamina and know-how to tap his hidden resources. He may enjoy the well-being which goes with a willing body. He will have trained his tenacity and patience, his initiative and fore-thought, his power of observation and his power of care. He will have developed steadfastness and he will be able to say "No" to the whims of the moment. He will have stimulated and nour-ished healthy interests until they become lively and deep, and perhaps develop into a passion. He will have discovered his strength and have begun to cure some of his weaknesses. The aver-age boy when first confronted with these tests will nearly always find some that look forbidding, almost hopelessly out of his reach, others he will find easy and appealing to his innate strength; but once he has started training he will be gripped by magic—a very simple magic, the magic of the puzzle...and he will struggle on against odds until one day he is winning in spite of some dis-ability. There always is some disability; but in the end he will triumph, turning defeat into victory, thus overcoming his own defeatism.

Kurt Hahn brought intensity to Outward Bound by asking difficult questions: "Can a demanding active service to their fellow man, in need and in danger, become an absorbing leisure activity for an ever increasing number of young people?" And he came up with difficult answers: "We need an aristocracy of service as an example to inspire others to do likewise."

Hahn said he wanted to introduce into the art of lifesaving the meticulous care which is generally devoted to the art of war, and he quoted William James to the effect that inspiration tends to evap-orate, leaving no trace on future conduct, unless it is translated into action. He suggested to Outward Bound that the secret of education was to teach young people the inner strength that comes from serving others. "There are three ways of trying to win the young. There's persuasion, there is compulsion, and there is attraction. You can preach at them, that is the hook without the worm; you can say 'you must volunteer,' that is of the devil; and you can tell them `you are need-ed,' that appeal hardly ever fails." He reasoned that "the experience of helping a fellow man in danger, or even of training in a realistic manner to be ready to give this help, tends to change the balance of power in a youth's inner life with the result that compassion can become the master motive."

Not long after leaving prison in Germany and just after founding Gordonstoun in Scotland, Hahn described the three essential approaches to education that he saw about him. He called them the Ionian, the Spartan and the Platonic. "The first believes that the individual ought to be nurtured and humored, regardless of the interests of the community. According to the second, the individ-ual may and should be neglected for the benefit of the State. The third, the Platonic view, believes that any nation is a slovenly guardian of its own interests if it does not do all it can to make the individual citizen discover his own powers. And it further believes that the individual becomes a cripple from his or her own point of view if he is not qualified by education to serve the community."

In school, Hahn asked his students to pledge themselves to the "training plan," establishing personal goals and a code of responsibility. Outward Bound instructors make a similar appeal to their students today—though not in the detailed terms used by Hahn at Salem and Gordonstoun,

Hahn asked his students to pledge themselves to the "training plan" establishing personal goals and a code of responsibility.

and it is a crucial aspect of the Outward Bound experience. The individual commitment of the student, the expressed desire to accomplish a worthy goal by means of the course, becomes, in effect, the moral basis of the community and the foundation both of compassion and of achievement.

Another important element that Hahn brought to Outward Bound was adventure—with all the risk it entails. He believed that education should cultivate a passion for life and that this can be accomplished only through experience, a shared sense of moment in the journey toward an exciting goal. Mountaineering and sailing were integral parts of his program at Gordonstoun and he made space in all his programs for student initiative—an expedition, a project, a sailing voyage. Hahn welcomed powerful emotions, such as awe, fear, exultant triumph. Part of his lifelong aspiration, part of the "whole" he sought through programs like Outward Bound, was to demonstrate that the experience accessible to any human being, at any level of ability, could be charged with joy and wonder in the doing.

Hahn also understood the educational value of working with small groups of students. He probably took this idea from military organization as it came into the youth movements of the late 19th century, especially the Scouting movement of Lord Baden-Powell in England. Hahn saw small groups as a way to develop the natural leadership abilities he thought were present in most people. Small groups require tremendous amounts of energy to reach the consensus necessary to meet objectives. Natural leaders emerge when the group must solve real problems instead of playing games with an unnatural reward system. Through this process a genuine community begins to appear.

A concern encompassing all the rest was Hahn's dedication to community service. As Hahn saw it, the link between individual and school depended for its meaning upon the link between school and society. This notion came into Outward Bound in the form of rescue service, and has since been applied across a broad spectrum of educational programming.

With such distinctive origins, it is only natural that Outward Bound should seek to ally itself more closely with conventional schooling. As the Outward Bound movement expanded after World War II, it was carried into the United States initially by educators such as Joshua L. Miner of Phillips Academy, Andover, and F. Charles Froelicher of Colorado Academy. From the 1960s through the 1970s, Outward Bound sought as an explicit aim to influence American schooling by persuading teachers and administrators to adapt experiential methods from the outdoor program to enhance formal learning.

The aim was not to manage such projects. Outward Bound turned over its ideas to school personnel for development within the schools, both public and private. For example, the Outward Bound schools set up teachers' courses and attempted to transmit ideals and methods in order to make an imprint on the dominant pattern of schooling for adolescents. The responses of participants from conventional schools emphasized the pedagogical vitality of experiential methods as well as the team-building and depth of mutual commitment elicited from students on Outward Bound courses. Studies of in-school adaptations produced some alternative models and promising but ambiguous results.

Beginning in the early 1970s, Project Adventure, an offshoot of Outward Bound started by instructors

---

Hahn saw small groups as a way to develop the natural leadership abilities he thought were present in most people.

wishing to work more closely with conventional schools, achieved success in applying experiential methods derived from Outward Bound to the schools. Project Adventure, which has been identified as an exemplary model by the National Diffusion Program of the U.S. Department of Education, went on to develop a repertoire of its own, paralleled by other creative offshoot programs, to assist schools in adventure programming, teacher training, and counseling.

By the mid-1970s, Outward Bound was part of a larger movement in the United States, referred to broadly as experiential education. The movement had some impact through generating alternative programs for adaptation by public and private schools, including not only outdoor education but such widely implemented strategies as action learning, experience-based career education, and cultural journalism. But while it had philosophical roots in common with these innovations, Outward Bound pursued a strategy of staying apart organizationally, mostly offering ideas and short-term training, then hoping that mainstream institutions would replicate what might prove most effective.

During the 80s, Outward Bound's direct involvement in schools and cities began to grow dramatically. The wilderness schools created urban programs in places like Baltimore, Atlanta, Portland (Maine), Chicago, Minneapolis, Denver, San Francisco and San Diego. In New York and Boston, Outward Bound created major urban centers each with its own permanent staff and boards of trustees. Funding from the DeWitt Wallace-Readers Digest Foundation made it possible for the national organization of Outward Bound to launch a nationwide initiative to support the growth of urban and educational programs based upon the pedagogies of Outward Bound. Subsequently, in the early 1990s, a design team sponsored by Outward Bound won a multimillion-dollar award from the New American Schools Development Corporation to foster "break the mold schools" following an "expeditionary learning" strategy drawn from the experience of Outward Bound. As the end of the century approaches, Outward Bound is well aware of its roots in the educational commitments of Kurt Hahn. These commitments are apparent not only in the provision of challenging, life-enhancing experiences through courses principally conducted in the outdoors, but also in a growing determination to transform everywhere the process of education, making it more active and more energized by the moral life of learning communities in action.

In the remainder of this chapter I would like to offer a personal interpretation of Kurt Hahn's vision of learning, one that attempts to connect the events of his life with his ideas. I believe it is this vision of Hahn's that shows most clearly what Outward Bound has to offer American education.

Kurt Hahn understood weakness better than strength. The goal of learning, in his view, was compensatory: to purify the destructive inclinations of the human personality, to redress the imbalances in modern ways of living, to develop each person's disabilities to their maximum potential, and to place new-found strength in service of those in need. Kurt Hahn was suspicious of presumed excellence; he paid scant attention to the glories of unsurpassed individual performance, whether it be on the playing fields at Eton or the examination ordeal of the German gymnasium. He understood, as few educators have so well, the tender fears of young people, their alienation before the rigors and rituals of adult power. He understood how wrong it was to defeat them with that power in order to make them learn. This strategy would only deepen their confusion about the meaning of their lives, making them cynical, lacking in humanity, even if it strengthened them. Hahn's favorite story was the Good Samaritan, wherein the strong, those clearly in a position to

> Kurt Hahn understood weakness better than strength. The goal of learning, in his view, was compensatory: to purify the destructive inclinations of the human personality, to redress the imbalances in modern ways of living, to develop each person's disabilities to their maximum potential, and to place new-found strength in service of those in need.

help the most, failed to act. It was the outsider, the weak, the despised who taught what it means to be a civilized human being.

Where did Hahn learn this, and if he once felt it himself, how did he convert his own weakness into an enduring vision of education? We must look, I believe, to that most tumultuous time of life to see the emerging center. In late adolescence, on the threshold of higher education and adult life, Hahn felt the impact of three events that changed his life.

The first was an expedition, some days of fresh air and majestic surroundings on a walking tour of the Dolomite Alps. One can well imagine the exhilaration of a boy in his teens on such a rite of passage. Famed for their bold, other-worldly shapes, their awe-inspiring hues of light and shadow from sunrise to sunset, the Dolomites imprinted on Hahn an inextinguishable love of natural beauty. As an educator, he would always be devising ways to turn his classrooms out of doors, putting his students into motion and forcing his teachers to come to grips with the healing powers of direct experience.

But something else happened on this expedition. A second event added to these other feelings a specific passion, strong enough to organize his self-discovery into a lifelong vocation. Two English schoolboys who accompanied Hahn gave him a gift, a book called *Emlohstobba* by the German educator Hermann Lietz. The title of the book was the name of their school, Abbotsholme, spelled backwards. Lietz wrote rapturously of life inside that school, where he served as master of studies for a sabbatical year under the innovative headmaster, Cecil Reddie. When Lietz returned to Germany, he fathered the country school movement there, inspiring others to begin schools more healthful for young people than the prevailing system of the time.

For Hahn this book was a momentous gift. Along with the living example of the two students from Abbotsholme, who impressed him with their healthy love of life and the sheer beauty of their alpine journey together, young Hahn must have felt in himself a new conviction of life's possibilities. Coming at a time when his own formal education was marching lockstep through the authoritarian, rigidly academic curriculum of the gymnasium, the alternative vision of a more humane and democratic school, capable of fostering more perfect human beings, seized his imagination with a force that can be judged only by abandoning strict chronology and looking ahead to the 70 indefatigable years of institution-building that lay ahead of him.

It was not on that trip, however, that Hahn imagined the school he hoped to build. Two years later, the year of his graduation from the gymnasium, a third event completed his initiation. He suffered the life-threatening sunstroke that permanently changed his life. Never again would he have the freedom to trek or sail long pleasurable distances out-of-doors. Nor was it certain, in the weeks following the accident, whether he would recover enough even to participate in normal functions of life. Depression set in, squelching his hopes. One would not be surprised if his boyhood dreams became cruel reminders of all that was not possible now. His life was a washout, a failure before it had really begun.

Here, and not in his later life of so many memorable accomplishments, the educational genius of the man is to be found. The center emerged as a discovery of who he really was inside, the gift of suddenly knowing what he had to do, and would do, when he bumped up against his own limitations.

As an educator, he would always be devising ways to turn his classrooms out of doors, putting his students into motion and forcing his teachers to come to grips with the healing powers of direct experience.

12

It was the scale of values, the plan of life, the desired future he asserted as his response to adversity when it came.

Adversity came to Hahn in several forms, all of which must have seemed insuperable from his perspective as he recovered in a darkened room from his accident . The physical disability would always be present in his life. It would be necessary for him to wear a broad-brimmed hat to protect his head from the sunlight. Frail in the heat, he would have to flee northward to a cooler climate in the summers. Periodically, he would need to undergo major operations to relieve the fluid pressure within his head. All this he knew, or could well imagine, in those months of convalescence.

In his darkened room, Kurt Hahn regenerated his spirit with a vision of what he could do with his life. He decided that he would someday start a school modeled on principles drawn from *Plato's Republic*, a school that would expand the wholesome influence he identified with Hermann Lietz and Cecil Reddie's Abbotsholme. How much of the vision came to him at that time and how much came later is not clear, but he grasped the essential outline. The school would harmonize the social and intellectual differences between its students by operating as a community of participation and active service. It would seek out the natural qualities of leadership, skill, and responsibility possessed by all in different ways when they see that they are truly needed. His school of the future would harmonize the wild and discordant personality of the adolescent by demonstrating that true need.

Once again, it is difficult to say how much of that vision became evident to Hahn during his recovery, and how much came to him as glimpses and inklings he later converted into plans and traditions. That the center emerged, though, is indisputable, both by his own account and because of the central place he gave to his thoughts during that dark night of the soul in later educational projects.

How could his vision be made believable to the alienated young? Closer to home, how could Kurt Hahn himself, in his debility and depression, bring himself to believe in a better life? Forced by the accident to reflect upon his own childhood, to seek out some deeper matrix of meaning to keep his spirits up, Hahn came face to face with his own youthful passion. That there exists, in everyone, a grand passion, an outlandish thirst for adventure, a desire to live boldly and vividly in the journey through life, sprang forth as the most salient lesson of his lifelong pedagogy.

That was not all, however, and it was not enough. For now the Dolomites and the classics flowed together to become Hahn's vision of the good. Dwelling for a time in his imagined world of Plato as he dreamed of a future school, feeling his spirit awakening to a great sense of purpose in that semi-darkness after the sunstroke, Hahn made the crucial connection. Passion must not be treated lightly. Its deep springs in human nature must not be poisoned. Above all, it must not be misdirected and turned to inhumane ends. The grand passion of the young must be embraced in wholesome ways by adult power. It must be nurtured instead of deformed or punished. Its creative force must be harnessed to the quest for a good society, the aim of Plato's educational designs. To accomplish this purpose would require more than a school in the traditional sense. Some separation from the existing human world, into the intensity of a journey-quest, confronting challenges and transforming opportunities for service, could change the balance of power in

> The school...would seek out the natural qualities of leadership, skill, and responsibility possessed by all in different ways when they see that they are truly needed.

young people, Hahn believed. Then they would be more inclined to use their lives, back in the world from which they came, to bring the good society into being.

With the center in view, the chronology of Kurt Hahn's life takes on greater meaning. Expelled from the land of his birth, the schoolmaster continued his career in Britain, which became a second homeland for him. When he opened Gordonstoun in 1934, Hahn carried the Salem tradition to the new setting, and he brought staff and students with him. New features appeared, such as the addition of rescue training to the service program. And some of the old practices changed, or were presented differently, in response to the cultural milieu of the British Isles. All this, of course, is to be expected in transplanting the design of an institution from one place and time to another. Certainly the transition was made easier by the strong affinity of Hahn's thinking with the traditions of Abbotsholme and the English public schools. What stands out, nonetheless, is the fact that Hahn was able in so short a time to create a new institution that, like his first school, would become known around the world for its distinctive educational practices.

If Hahn had not been restless, if he had not felt driven toward wider applications of his principles beyond any school he might ever create, he would perhaps have settled down to a long career as the eccentric headmaster of a school favored by the English aristocracy. But he was not satisfied. He began to organize a constellation of other educational forms around Gordonstoun, using the school as a staging ground for programs through which he hoped to instruct the whole society around him in the first lessons of sound living and civic responsibility. The Moray Badge Scheme took form in 1936, followed quickly by the larger and better known County Badge a year later.

Along the way, Hahn experimented with short courses to discover the combination of challenging experiences that might help young people discover new ways of organizing their lives and working with other people. In 1941, with Lawrence Holt, Hahn started Outward Bound as a short course. Initially, the goal was to strengthen the will of young men so that they could prevail against adversity as Great Britain faced staggering losses at sea during World War II. After the program had demonstrated its effectiveness, it continued to expand during the postwar years, furnishing opportunities for personal and social growth to many people beyond the original clientele of boys and young men.

Chronology alone cannot account for Hahn's widening sphere of educational activity. Only by grasping how he continued to draw both from a sense of weakness and from the strong idealism at the center of his being can we understand his intuitive leaps as he created new programs over the years. Hahn perceived clearly that schools as we know them are not equal to the urgent problems of social life in this century. Even the best schools probably damage as much as develop the volatile inner lives of young people.

One reason for this unintended consequence is that schools represent only a partial solution to a much more pervasive problem. The problem of how to educate the whole person cannot be solved without learning how to civilize human communities, which in turn cannot be done without preparing the entire world society in the art of living harmoniously at the highest levels of potential activity and understanding. Hahn's debt to Plato was his conviction that education must embrace all these aspects of human life. A vision of what is most desirable in education must embody not only some notion of how the whole is to be organized, but what it will take for that

Hahn perceived clearly that schools as we know them are not equal to the urgent problems of social life in this century. Even the best schools probably damage as much as develop the volatile inner lives of young people.

whole to be good. Without a vision of wholeness, without at least a hope that the compassionate community might someday be realized on a worldwide scale, people are not inclined to live on humane terms with one another.

Exiled to the British Isles, Kurt Hahn was restless at the center of his being. Carrying with him an unflinching impression of the expanding Third Reich and its effects on European civilization, he could never be satisfied with the auspicious beginning of a single school. Soon after his arrival he began to write and speak in public, deploring the general lack of fitness among the British people. He urged his hosts to recognize the need for programs on a large scale that would combine individual training plans with group projects to build stronger civic consciousness.

Out of such concerns he initiated the Moray and County Badge Schemes. The latter quickly expanded and became further elaborated in many counties across the British Isles, spreading even to other countries in the British Commonwealth. The County Badge granted public recognition to young people who completed a planned course of challenges. They first adopted a training plan of physical conditioning and personal health habits. Then they undertook an arduous expedition requiring group decision making as well as individual effort. They also completed a project demanding new skills and craftsmanship. Finally, they engaged in service activities, experiencing the value of compassion through direct action on behalf of the community or specific people in need.

At the beginning of the war, the County Badge contained most of the essential features of the Outward Bound program as it would develop in future years. Indeed, the secretary and key promoter of the County Badge Experimental Committee, James Hogan, became the first warden of the first Outward Bound School at Aberdovey, In Wales. Yet there was a difference, and it was more than the residential setting and month-long sustained program of Outward Bound. Although both programs offered models for changing how individuals organized their lives, there was something more universal and enduring about Outward Bound.

Hahn had realized how close are weakness and strength in the most powerful forms of education. In his own day, he perceived clearly, while others did not, the subtle line that distinguishes compassionate service from destructive egotism. On the one hand, he feared the lack of will among those whose lives stood in the path of the advancing Third Reich. Hence his call for programs like the County Badge to build fitness and commit young people to civic ideals. But on the other hand, he recognized the affinity between his methods and those of the Nazis, one used for the good, the other for deadly ends.

There is an irony in this affinity, since Hahn was criticized by some in England for importing the para-military methods of the Hitler Youth. The irony is that the Hitler Youth movement did not invent the intensive methods of socialization they used to unleash the energies of the young. Rather, they borrowed from the leading educators of the day and applied the methods to their own goals. Hahn knew this well, for he had seen the Hitler Youth before he left Germany. Their leaders had adapted and twisted to demonic purposes the training plan of Salem. Hahn had witnessed, therefore, the effects of reaching the whole person with the fascist plan of life instead of a Samaritan ethic. Hitler and his followers were reinforcing the passion of the young, giving them a spirit of adventure, introducing them to self-development and cooperation in the outdoors, then

Hahn had realized how close are weakness and strength in the most powerful forms of education. In his own day, he perceived clearly, while others did not, the subtle line that distinguishes compassionate service from destructive egotism.

Historical

giving them meaningful opportunities to serve. Hahn recognized that there was no time for complacency. The weakness of the status quo must be acknowledged. All education must be made activist, or else the humane values upon which western democracies were built would succumb to a determined usurper.

Not even in its desperate beginnings before the onslaught of the Third Reich did Outward Bound ever train young people for war, but it arose fully conscious of the challenge presented by the Hitler Youth, that nationwide mobilization of young people to serve the cause of world conquest and genocide. Never did anyone press Outward Bound toward becoming a preparation for violence, and in this respect it would always remain distinct from youth mobilizations under totalitarian regimes. Yet it is difficult to imagine how Outward Bound would ever have come into being if it had not been for Hahn's recognition of the weakness of democratic cultures before well-organized forms of authoritarian education that were appallingly efficient at stirring up the passions of the young for collective violence.

Through Outward Bound, Hahn hoped to foster a deeper intensity of commitment in the rite of passage from youth to adult life. He was intent on creating more dramatic challenges and victories for the young than were available in conventional forms of schooling. Advocating a more arduous quest than was present in the institutions around him, Hahn was working from a disability greater than his own, a collective predicament verging on catastrophe. In England during the German blitzkrieg, it was by no means apocalyptic to argue that there would need to be a new education, reconstructed on a massive scale, to produce the compassionate army needed to preserve what was left of civilization at home. Hahn believed that an intensive program of training, expedition, reflection and service could make a difference.

That belief survived beyond the exigencies of war, but Hahn's own direct role quickly receded once the philosophical values were in place to launch Outward Bound. While Hahn continued to influence Outward Bound, it soon took on a life of its own under the vigorous leadership of many people drawn to its idealism and hardy lifestyle over the years. Taking an image from Plato, Hahn likened himself to a midwife of educational projects as he sparked ideas for new endeavors and then left much of the development and maintenance to others. Outward Bound sea and mountain schools proliferated across several continents in the following decades. As it adapted itself to different cultures in later years, Outward Bound lost its wartime urgency, but it maintained a zest for adventure and Hahn's legacy of moral purpose.

Outward Bound has come to mean many things in different places and for the great variety of people who are drawn to it, but at its heart, in every time and place, is Hahn's own center, his conviction that it is possible, even in a relatively short time, to introduce greater balance and compassion into human lives by impelling people into experiences that show them they can rise above adversity and overcome their own defeatism, make more of their lives than they thought they could, and learn to serve others with their strength.

Hahn's postwar contributions include several other projects of which he considered himself more midwife than instigator. It would be most accurate to characterize him as the moving spirit, since his art of persuasion was decisive in each case. The Trevelyan Scholarships, for example, provided funds for young people to attend Oxford and Cambridge based on experiential as well as academic

Through Outward Bound, Hahn hoped to foster a deeper intensity of commitment in the rite of passage from youth to adult life. He was intent on creating more dramatic challenges and victories for the young than were available in conventional forms of schooling.

criteria: Applicants were asked to complete a project of their own design, which would be reviewed by a selection panel. Shortly after a recurrence of his sunstroke in the early 1950s, Hahn helped to launch the Duke of Edinburgh Award, a program similar to the County Badge but more widely developed throughout the British Commonwealth. His crowning achievement after the war was the United World Colleges, which began with the founding of Atlantic College in 1962.

If Outward Bound's origins are to be found in the war, those of the United World Colleges appear in the desire to build institutions that will offer a living example of what it means to be at peace. Taking students from ages 16 to 19, equivalent to the sixth form in England or the last two years before post secondary education in the United States, these colleges bring together boys and girls from all over the world, from competing social and economic systems, from rivaling cultures and religions. The program fosters world citizenship, an interconnected leadership of people who have experienced a collective life of active dialogue and peacemaking service. The curriculum, like that of Gordonstoun, combines both academic and experiential challenges, but the institutions have developed in new directions under their diverse leadership, leaving some of Hahn's educational practices behind while preserving others. Kurt Hahn's original insight, that such institutions were possible, stands as perhaps the greatest legacy of his influence as they continued to thrive and expand in the 1980s.

Returning to Germany for his last days, Kurt Hahn died near Salem, in Hermannsberg, on December 14, 1974. The entry in Britain's *Dictionary of National Biography* calls him "headmaster and citizen of humanity." Hahn's educational influence persists under such organizations as the Round Square Conference, which includes schools modeled on Salem and Gordonstoun. His genius in devising short-term educational experiences has not stopped infusing energy and inspiration into the Outward Bound Trust, which oversees Outward Bound schools throughout the world. His love of peace flourishes in the United World Colleges, not to mention the many other institutions and individuals who continue to embody his ideals. The man's educational vision remains, beckoning like an adventure, arising from weakness to teach about strength, turning self-discovery into acts of compassion, everywhere defending human decency.

The man's educational vision remains, beckoning like an adventure, arising from weakness to teach about strength, turning self-discovery into acts of compassion, everywhere defending human decency.

CHAPTER 2

Theory Into Practice: The Pedagogies of Experience

Courage: The power to let go of the familiar

— Raymond Lindquist

It is not because things are difficult that we do not dare,
it is because we do not dare that they are difficult.

— Seneca

Education has always drawn nourishment from experience. One learned what one lived and the collective experience and wisdom of cultures were handed down from one generation to the next through play and formal and informal apprenticeships.

In time, society and the scope and nature of essential knowledge became so complex that systems were established to transmit knowledge in a more efficient manner than apprenticeships could do. Teachers were led to dispense information rather than encourage the pursuit of knowledge. In *Pedagogy of the Oppressed,* Paulo Friere refers to this as the "Banking Concept" of education. The key assumption being that a mind, like a bank vault, is a receptacle passively awaiting a deposit.

As socio-economic powers shifted toward assembly-line manufacturing, similar models of production were codified for schools. Thus legions of students were moved through an educational system much as cars were moved through an assembly plant.

Yet the world has changed. In the United States, the industrial society has given way to the post-industrial "Information Age," where the marketable resource is knowledge and the product of effort is information. In such a society information is readily available; it is experience that is a scarce commodity.

Outward Bound addresses this with a straightforward proposition: Learn through experience, but not just *any* experience. Outward Bound's pedagogy takes great care to impel students into value-forming experiences—experiences that illustrate truths about the world, its people, places, things and ideas. In Outward Bound a high value is placed on physical as well as mental and emotional experiences, and on thoughtful reflection upon them. The experiences are consequential, and framed within the context of individual initiative, teamwork, compassion and service.

Application

Photo Left: **Lessons learned in ropes course exercises will have direct transference to the classroom.**

The Elements of Outward Bound Education

The Teacher: Teachers should expect and guide students to take responsibility, lead and learn. They should know more and do less. They should have more content knowledge about academic subjects, pedagogical practices, curricula, human development, group development, communication and counseling; yet they should not lecture or give too much information or guidance. They should encourage students to assume more active and direct responsibility for their own education and be involved enough to insure the students' physical and emotional safety, monitor and guide the group, and assure the academic and philosophical integrity of lessons.

The Experience: An Outward Bound lesson typically starts with concrete experiences and then builds to abstractions. A writing lesson on "trees" would first place students in a forest—touching, smelling, measuring and examining trees in all sorts of ways. It would have them visit a lumber yard, an orchard or tree farm, thin a plant or prune trees as part of a forest management service project, or inventory trees in and around the school or community.

The potency of this general sequence of an experiential lesson is strengthened when the experiences are such that: (1) The task is relevant, thus there must be a meaningful purpose behind the activity, as in real-world applications. (2) The task has clear short and long-term outcomes known and understood by the learner. (3) Multiple routes to meaningful outcomes are available. (4) The learner is empowered to construct emotional and intellectual meanings. (5) Learnings build upon learnings.

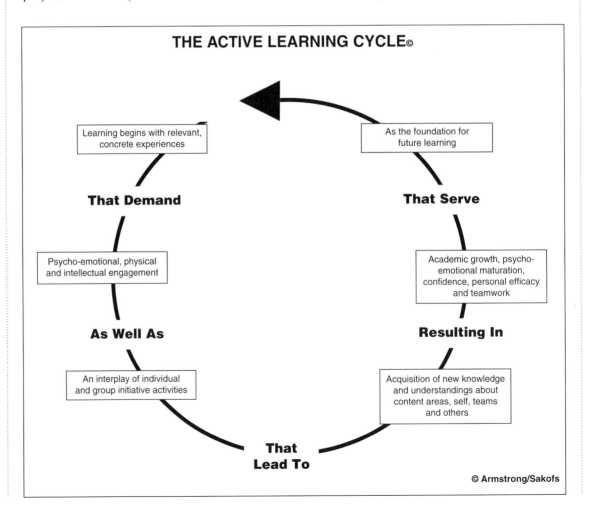

THE ACTIVE LEARNING CYCLE©

Learning begins with relevant, concrete experiences

As the foundation for future learning

That Demand

That Serve

Psycho-emotional, physical and intellectual engagement

Academic growth, psycho-emotional maturation, confidence, personal efficacy and teamwork

As Well As

Resulting In

An interplay of individual and group initiative activities

Acquisition of new knowledge and understandings about content areas, self, teams and others

That Lead To

© Armstrong/Sakofs

Immediate, Consequential Applications of Knowledge: In a traditional physics class, concepts involving friction and angles would be taught with books and then tested with experiments in a laboratory. In Outward Bound classrooms, students experience, then discuss, then experience again in a living laboratory in which the consequences matter. For example, in rock climbing and in particular the safety systems used in rock-climbing, knot tying is an essential skill illustrative of concepts involving friction and angles. If a traditional educational program incorporated a climbing experience into its curriculum it would, no doubt, be found in physical education and the teacher would spend a significant amount of classroom time teaching various knots in preparation for the experience. In an Outward Bound classroom, the instructor would bring the knot-tying lesson to the rock-climbing site at a time when the group is about to engage in rock climbing, when the need to know is a powerful tool focusing the student's attention on the skill to be learned. Moreover, in the Outward Bound classroom, the physics and physical education teachers might team teach to integrate disiplines to maximize learning.

Time for Solitude and Reflection: Reflection can be a solitary activity, a group activity or anything in between. In Outward Bound formal time is set aside for the student to be alone during an activity known as the "solo." Solos can range from a few hours to a few days; the length of time is predetermined and understood by students and teachers. In preparation for a solo, instructors may pose questions for students to consider, and thus orient them in the reflective process.

Reflection can be done individually at any time and in large or small group settings. It is essential to promoting deeper and clearer learnings. The reflective process will yield insights and learning that must be given an opportunity to be tested and refined by creating more opportunities for the learner to apply knowledge and insights. Allow students to engage in new experiences that build on previous learnings.

Adventure: Adventure is essential. Webster's defines adventure as "exciting and sometimes dangerous activities that are remembered." There is an element of physical and emotional challenge in Outward Bound activities and lessons. Some of them have a high degree of perceived risk: One of the teacher's most important functions is to insure that the actual risk is very small while the perceived risk may be very high.

Physical Fitness, Metaphorical Significance and Teamwork: Outward Bound activities such as rock climbing and mountaineering have intrinsic value as recreational pursuits and help develop participants' strength, balance and coordination.

They also help develop teamwork by creating interdependencies, thus demonstrating the value of collaboration. In rock climbing, the climber depends on the belayer to ensure safety, and by rotating roles, trust-based relationships form as each must climb and belay.

These activities also have useful metaphorical potential. The challenge of climbing a sheer rock wall is significant in itself; but it can also serve as a concrete manifestation of the many obstacles that confront and challenge us throughout our lives. It is how we react to these obstacles that determines the nature of our experience of life. The encounter with the rock is also an encounter with the self; it can serve as a vehicle for self-examination and self-discovery.

Expeditionary Learning Outward Bound Designed Principles

In 1992, a request for proposals for "break the mold" K-12 schools from the New American Schools Development Corporation, a privately-supported initiative of major U.S. corporations and the federal government, encouraged Outward Bound to formulate an explicit set of educational principles from its experience and the educational thought and writings of Kurt Hahn.[1]

Principle 1: The Primacy of Self-Discovery — Learning happens best with emotion, challenge and the requisite support. People discover their abilities, values, "grand passions," and responsibilities in situations that offer adventure and the unexpected. They must have tasks that require perseverance, fitness, craftsmanship, imagination, self-discipline and significant achievement. A primary job of the educator is to help students overcome their fear and discover they have more in them than they think.

Principle 2: The Having of Wonderful Ideas — Teach so as to build on children's curiosity about the world by creating learning situations that provide matter to think about, time to experiment, and time to make sense of what is observed. Foster a community in which students' and adults' ideas are respected.

Principle 3: The Responsibility for Learning — Learning is both a personal, individually specific process of discovery and a social activity. Each of us learns within and for ourselves and as part of a group. Every aspect of a school must encourage children, young people, and adults to become increasingly responsible for directing their own personal and collective learning.

Principle 4: Intimacy and Caring — Learning is fostered best in small groups where there is trust, sustained caring and mutual respect among all members of the learning community. Keep schools and learning groups small. Be sure there is a caring adult looking after the progress of each child. Arrange for the older students to mentor the younger ones.

Principle 5: Success and Failure — All students must be assured a fair measure of success in learning in order to nurture the confidence and capacity to take risks and rise to increasingly difficult challenges. But it is also important to experience failure, to overcome negative inclinations, to prevail against adversity and to learn to turn disabilities into opportunities.

1. Informed by Kurt Hahn's *Seven Laws of Salem*, by Paul Ylvisaker's *The Missing Dimension* and by Eleanor Duckworth's *The Having of Wonderful Ideas and Other Essays on Teaching and Learning.* New York: Teachers College Press, 1987.

Principle 6: Collaboration and Competition — Teach so as to join individual and group development so that values of friendship, trust, and group endeavor are made manifest. Encourage students to compete, not against each other, but with their own personal best and with rigorous standards of excellence.

Principle 7: Diversity and Inclusivity — Diversity and inclusivity in all groups dramatically increases richness of ideas, creative power, problem-solving ability, and acceptance of others. Encourage students to investigate, value and draw upon their own different histories, talents and resources, together with those of other communities and cultures. Keep the schools and learning groups heterogeneous.

Principle 8: The Natural World — A direct and respectful relationship with the natural world refreshes the human spirit and reveals the important lessons of recurring cycles and cause and effect. Students learn to become stewards of the earth and of the generations to come.

Principle 9: Solitude and Reflection — Solitude, reflection and silence replenish our energies and open our minds. Be sure students have time alone to explore their own thoughts, make their own connections and create their own ideas. Then give the opportunity to exchange their reflections with each other and with adults.

Principle 10: Service and Compassion — We are crew, not passengers, and are strengthened by acts of consequential service to others. One of a school's primary functions is to prepare its students with attitudes and skills to learn from and be of service to others.

Establishing the Context for Active Learning: Four Building Blocks

The form and structure of an Outward Bound classroom will be very different from most traditional classrooms. Active learning requires more flexibility; it is sometimes noisier, sometimes more spontaneous, and sometimes more physical.

But it need not be disruptive, unruly, out-of-control or devoid of content. Rather, if structured properly, classes can be well managed and content rich.

The First Building Block — Goals and Objectives
It is critically important that the goals and objectives for a class be clearly and explicitly stated. This way everyone knows what they are involved in. Roles and responsibilities of all class members should be clearly stated and reflect Hahn's notion that "we are crew not passengers."

The Second Building Block — Model The Model
The foundation of the classroom is not the activities, but the humanity and spirit with which they are conducted. Teachers should be clear about the fundamental qualities they wish to promote, and model those qualities themselves in ways that communicate their importance.

The Third Building Block — Physical and Emotional Safety
When people feel threatened or unsafe, their energies are focused on addressing the source of their discomfort or concern. It is difficult if not impossible for students to focus on the learning goals established within a school when they are focused on their own safety.

Some of the activities associated with the Outward Bound Classroom require special attention to safety. Teachers must understand the activities they will be using and the safety issues associated with them.

If you intend to move out of your classroom to use the educational potential of the school building, its grounds and the surrounding community, then you must also know about these areas. How safe are they? Where are the police stations, firehouses and other emergency services located? Are there other dangers, such as power lines, garbage and debris, construction sites, heavy traffic or bodies of water? What are the social dangers?

Like physical dangers, teachers must also attend to the emotional concerns of their students. Emotional safety is intimately tied to the climate of the classroom and the existence of guiding principles that reinforce and support the risk-taking and personal disclosure associated with active learning. Students should be able to feel they can take risks, such as "dare to be stupid" when asking questions or trying to understand an issue; students should feel safe about expressing their true opinions about the broad spectrum of issues that surface in class; they should feel safe enough to share who they are and what they think, feel and believe.

The Forth Building Block — A Classroom Covenant
The first element of the Classroom Covenant is "Challenge by Choice." Coined by our colleagues at Project Adventure, it is the idea that students have the responsibility and right to engage in activities to the degree they feel comfortable. The second element, also developed by Project

Adventure, is the "Full Value Contract," an agreement between participants to commit themselves to getting the most out of the experiences presented, with the intention to respect the contributions of each participant.

With a commitment on the part of the students to try, complemented by the understanding that their engagement is by choice and that they have the right to withdraw from an activity, the stage is set for powerful learning to occur.

Outward Bound's Keys to Creating a Successful Teaching and Learning Environment

1. Clearly express the goals and objectives of the class, its operating principles and the rules governing all interactions.

2. Model the appropriate behaviors, attitudes and principles to create the proper context for learning.

3. Identify the full spectrum of safety concerns associated with active learning so that the students can be emotionally and physically free to maximize the opportunities to learn.

4. Create a classroom operating agreement that embraces the elements of the Classroom Covenant.

Common Practices in Outward Bound Active Learning Applicable to the Classroom

This section introduces eight programmatic constructs used in many Outward Bound activities. They are introduced for they constitute constructs that can be used to enhance the power of initiative activities. But note, too, that they are versatile constructs that can also be used in a broad spectrum of ways to enhance the quality of individual activities, lessons large and small, as well as entire thematic curricula units. The eight constructs presented below are: the Circle up, Brief, Debrief, Solo, Journaling, Rotating Leadership, Celebration and Holistic Engagement.

Circle Up: The circle Up is a protocol used in Outward Bound programs to bring people together and it entails having the group form a circle or ring. Standing or sitting is acceptable and should serve the needs of the group. The circle is used because structurally it has no predetermined leadership position, and because it helps focus the group within itself. Likewise, the circle also makes it easy for team-members to see and speak with each other.

Within Outward Bound, the Circle Up is often used to launch an activity, end an activity, or regroup and refocus team-members when it is required or requested. Often when people Circle Up, they move physically closer to each other. This, in turn, stands as a physical statement of the bonding that is sought.

Briefing & Framing: Briefing is a way which team members can be presented with the scope and nature of their challenge. Most often it is a conversation, but briefings can be done through mime, pictures or in other creative ways. Certain briefings may take a few minutes and simply describe the rules of a game; others may outline the full scope and nature of an entire curricular unit. The instructor might use the briefing to introduce a certain context in which the group might approach the task at hand. In Outward Bound this context is the framing of a challenge. For example, when introducing the activity known as The Wall, one way to frame the challenge is to do the circle up and have the instructor talk about how we all are challenged by obstacles in our work and personal lives. And it is how we approach these obstacles, i.e., with resignation, negativity or a sheer dogged persistence, that will ultimately determine our successes. The instructor then asks the group to view the wall, and the challenge to surmount it, as a metaphor for the challenges in their own lives. Thus, how will they meet the challenge and succeed? Upon whom will they depend? How will they ask for help? Also, are there people in their lives who are facing challenges and who could use their support, guidance or assistance? Once the challenge is framed, the group is then given a few minutes to reflect on the challenge before they attempt the wall.

Debriefing: Debriefing refers to the mechanisms by which team-members are provided with an opportunity to reflect on, analyze and discuss any aspect of an activity. During a Debrief, process and product issues are fair game for discussion. Debriefs can be held in almost any format: whole group, small group, or one-on-one. They may involve the leader or teacher; or may be a forum for students to engage each other. Within the context of a suppotative team and using communication skills learned, during a Debrief people often explore their own behavior or issues around group functioning as well as substantive issues related to the challenge itself. When Debriefs involve the entire group, they are often conducted in a Circle Up.

Journaling: The journal is a tool students can use to keep a personal record of events, learnings and insights. It is a place for them to reflect on product and process, their own efficacy and other issues or concerns—large or small. It is a place for insights to find expression; for writing and drawing and musing.

Solo: We have learned that the power of Outward Bound programs is augmented by providing students with time to be alone, think, reflect, and consider the lessons learned. Solos can be held at any time of the day or night, and can be as simple as a moment of silence or as extensive as long periods of solitude. At Gordonstoun, Kurt Hahn provided each of his students with an opportunity to enjoy at least one half-hour of solitude a week; one hour, half-day and multi-day solos are often incorporated into Outward Bound programs.

Rotating Leadership: Whatever the subject of study, in Outward Bound lessons are structured to provide students with opportunities to both lead and follow. For those whose personalities do not naturally bring them to positions of authority, they are encouraged to lead and make decisions. Likewise, for those who are used to asserting themselves into positions of leadership, there is great learning potential for them in positions of followership. To assure that these benefits are realized, in Outward Bound programs we employ the practice of Rotating Leadership among classmates.

Celebration: Celebration of accomplishments is an integral part of all Outward Bound programs. It bonds people together, affirms accomplishments, and makes people feel good. Though celebrations can be planned and formal, in Outward Bound they often erupt spontaneously with laughter and cheers, thus punctuating learning and activity with moments of joy.

Holistic Engagement: The philosophical underpinnings of Outward Bound education embraces the notion that learning is a complex, dynamic interplay between all aspects of the human experience. Thus it is intellectual and physical; rational and emotional; concrete and abstract; joyful and frustrating; tedious and exciting; noisy and quiet; active and sedentary; and the list goes on. Outward Bound educators recognize these relationships, and through the various activities presented encourage students to embrace and appreciate learning in its multifaceted beauty.

CHAPTER 3

Integrating Outward Bound
into Traditional School Settings

> *The journey of a thousand miles*
> *begins with one step*
> — LAO-TZU

It is easier to talk a good game in education than it is to play one. The real world practicalities of many schools make it difficult for our ideas and visions to find expression in lasting programs. For the philosophies and principles of Outward Bound to be successfully translated into real experiences for the school community there are many practical concerns that must be addressed. Fifty minute periods, teacher isolation, transportation needs, tight school budgets, student expectations, and pressure from parents, administrators and other teachers can all present challenges to innovation, experiential approaches to teaching and learning. This chapter provides strategies for dealing with these practical concerns of bringing Outward Bound into our schools and classrooms.

Developing the school campus

Outward Bound programs and values can potentially have an impact on all members of a school community. These programs can take many forms and be targeted at a variety of groups and purposes. There is a need for the adults in the school community to build mutual respect, trust, and a sense of team identity. Students need programs that address their affective and social development, and build a sense of efficacy. And the learning process needs to be infused with more adventure and engagement. Outward Bound can help meet these needs within schools through programs such as the following:

- Multi-day wilderness, or urban wilderness experiences for students, faculty, administrators and staff;
- Community service programs;
- Initiatives, new games, or ropes course activities that:
  - augment existing physical education classes;
  - offer corporate-style team building workshops for various school groups;
  - punctuate student or faculty retreats and planning meetings
  - train students in the affective and social skills needed to succeed with experiential learning styles;

Special thanks to Scott Hartl, Expeditionary Learning Outward Bound, for writing this chapter.

Implementation

- Offer an adventure-based leadership or citizenship class;
- Form a student wilderness outing club;
- Form a student service club that focuses on identifying and working to meet loca community needs;
- Run adventure-based multi- or single-day programs as part of a freshman orientation program; and,
- Take a hands-on project and activity-centered approach to teaching academic classes to create the sense of adventure, responsibility, cooperation, and consequence that characterize more traditional Outward Bound experiences and give them their sense of vitality and personal significance.

All of these applications of Outward Bound have been used extensively within school settings for many years. The specifics of the programs and experiences that are offered in any given school will reflect that school's individual needs. Using this approach, a small group of interested teachers and I "worked to integrate Outward Bound pedagogues, values and experiences into the small urban high school which we taught."

- First we offered programs for teachers and administrators. Two, five-day trips run by the Hurricane Island Outward Bound School were designed to orient interested faculty and administrators to the Outward Bound process. These initial trips allowed faculty and administrators to experience Outward Bound directly and served as a forum for team building and for brainstorming ways we could apply what we were experiencing in our school district. The value of these trips cannot be overstated.
- The following year we offered three-day wilderness experiences for small groups of students and teachers. The participants were usually all from one particular class. These trips took many forms and were run in environments ranging from camp settings with cabins and shower facilities to winter backpacking trips in which we camped in tents and plowed through two-foot snowstorms. These trips were designed to provide a shared adventure experience through which the class could develop relationships, trust, teamwork, and an identity as a group.
- Day trips were offered at several points during the year to these students to serve as refresher experiences and continue their development of affective and social skills. These trips included rock climbing as a creative writing vehicle for English classes, group initiative exercises and new games, caving trips for geology classes, fresh water ecology excursions using a rowing barge for transportation, ropes course experiences, and day hikes in the mountains.
- The student government, for which I served as advisor, used group initiative exercises, ropes courses, and outdoor adventures as part of their leadership training and to punctuate planning retreats.
- A half-year adventure-based leadership class was offered as an elective. This class employed service projects, ropes course and rock-climbing activities, and initiative exercises to prepare the students for a culminating activity in which the high school students designed and implemented a four-week program with fifth graders to build their self-esteem and address the challenges of peer pressure and drug and alcohol use. This class was very popular and received a great response from parents.
- The Outward Bound spin-off program in our school, that was arguably the most effective and has reached the largest number of students, was started by a tenth grader named Jim.

Take a hands-on project and activity-centered approach to teaching academic classes to create the sense of adventure, responsibility, cooperation, and consequence which characterize more traditional Outward Bound experiences and give them their sense of vitality and personal significance.

Jim had dropped out of school and was eventually enrolled in a thirty-day Outward Bound course. Jim re-entered school the next year and approached me about staring an Outing Club that would do "Outward Bound stuff." Jim was president of the Outing Club for three years, and under his leadership it grew to include over fifty members and run at least ten trips each year. The outing club found great favor with the school administration due to its success in offering some of the behaviorally tougher students in the school a positive outlet for their energies.

For a large percentage of students, experiences such as those listed above were the most meaningful and remembered experiences of their school year. These experiences, however, served only as punctuation. The need for a fuller program soon became clear. I witnessed many students return from Outward Bound experiences filled with a "seize the day" attitude and full of resolve to keep the fire going. Too often these students fell quickly back into old patterns, having failed to transfer the skills and attitudes developed while on Outward Bound to their everyday school lives. This lack of transference is understandable considering the limited role to which students are relegated in many classes. Outward Bound experiences serve as high-impact training for students in the values of perseverance, cooperation, initiative, compassion, and responsibility. However if a student returns to classes that require her only to take notes and process second-hand information provided by teachers, books, and videos, these values will soon begin to atrophy. If we are to have a lasting impact on our students we must learn how to teach our English, science, social studies, math, and other academic subjects through curricula that offer students the same sense of adventure, responsibility, and consequence that create vitality and personal relevance in Outward Bound experiences.

Anchoring the everyday experience of students in a learning style that offers a sense of adventure, responsibility, cooperation, and consequence is a difficult but worthy challenge. Teaching is a craft. Consequently, each teacher's personal style will inform his approach to embedding Outward Bound values in the teaching of his classes. There are, however, some general principles which teachers can use to guide and inform the integration of Outward Bound values with the teaching of academic classes. These general principles are as follows:

- As part of the orientation to the class or school the teacher(s) and students participate in a shared adventurous activity to begin building a sense of community and trust in the classroom.
- Classes are designed to explore a limited number of topics deeply and focus on the process of learning rather than focusing on "covering" a wide breadth of material. If possible the students' core classes are linked by common themes.
- Intellectually and physically engaing projects are a key feature of the curriculum in all classes. Quality projects provide opportunities for students to learn and apply important knowledge and skills and provide an answer to the question of "why are we learning this?" by being crafted to meet the real needs or interests of the student, classroom, school or community.
- The teacher acts as coach, collaborator and guide rather than boss or repository and filter of knowledge.
- Partnerships with outside "experts" in the field that the students are exploring are sought. Outside experts can help to deepen student understanding, provide a voice other than the teacher and raise standards for their work by exposing them to the work of professionals in the field.

> **Outward Bound experiences serve as high-impact training for students in the values of perseverance, cooperation, initiative, compassion, and responsibility. However if a student returns to classes that require her only to take notes and process second-hand information provided by teachers, books, and videos, these values will soon begin to atrophy.**

- Field work is used to punctuate classroom learning.
- Portfolio and performance assessment methods are used. Criteria for good work is discussed with students and modeled for them on an on-going basis and the skill of critique and revision are practiced to help students get more from themselves than they knew was possible.
- Students exhibt and present their work to an audience beyond the teacher.

The features listed above place the student at the center of the learning process and create a sense of adventure in the classroom. Students are active. They are engaged physically as well as intellectually through hands-on projects and activities. The role of the teacher is to create learning environments or situations that impel students into action through the perception of real consequences beyond grades or disciplinary action. The teacher then acts as coach, collaborator, or guide during the learning process and enables students to solve their own problems as they arise. Student investment is enhanced by providing for choice, within a determined structure, concerning what and how they are going to learn. And the work that the students do is shared with a community larger than the classroom. This may be done through student-produced publications, inviting local experts in to help evaluate student work, having students present their work orally or on videotape, or targeting work to address real needs of others in the school or local community.

When content is taught through hands-on projects and activities there needs to be structured time for students to reflect on both the content and process of their learning. This reflective time facilitates connections to broader concepts and helps students gain mastery in the basic skills of learning. Portfolio assessment and reflective journals are strong vehicles for facilitating student reflection.

Some of the deepest work with the style of teaching and learning that I have so briefly described above is being done by the hundreds of teachers involved with Expeditionary Learning Outward Bound schools throughout the country. Teachers and students in Expeditionary Learning schools spend most of their days in school embarked on purposeful, rigorous "learning expeditions" which include strong intellectual, service and physical dimensions. Learning expeditions are being practiced in grades kindergarten through twelve and are sustained, in-depth studies of a single theme or topic which generally take 4-9 weeks and are the core of the curriculum. Projects and performances which include purposeful fieldwork are the center of each expedition. The central office of Expeditionary Learning Outward Bound is in Cambridge MA.

Working with adults: Parents, Teachers, and Administrators

Programs can flourish only where there is an atmosphere of mutual respect, trust, and a sense of common mission. Consequently, educators working to bring active learning into their schools and classrooms must attend to creating the prerequisite conditions for program growth. This means working with the adults in the system e.g., the teachers, administrators, and parents.

Some thoughts on teaming
If this chapter had to be written in one word, that word would be "teaming." Teaming a group of like-minded teachers into a school-within-a-school or "house" structure is one way to address many of the constraining factors facing teachers as they work to implement Outward Bound

> **If this chapter had to be written in one word, that word would be "teaming." Teaming a group of like minded teachers into a school-within-a-school or "house" structure is one way to address many of the constraining factors facing teachers as they work to implement Outward Bound programs within their school and classes.**

programs within their school and classes. Teaming can take many forms: from a fully autonomous situation in which all classes are covered for the group of students within the team, to a core team in which the students have three- or four-team classes that are scheduled contiguously to create a significant block of time, to the least committing situation in which a group of students' schedules are simply linked to ensure that they all have the same teachers. To reap the maximum benefits from a teaming situation the following structural elements are paramount:

- A significant block of contiguous time is created, such as a morning or an afternoon, for team classes;
- Team teachers have their rooms adjoining or in close proximity to one another; and,
- Team teachers all have common planning time.

The creation of large contiguous time blocks for team classes offers a way around the constraints of fifty-minute periods. The team can use its time block creatively to facilitate the use of extended projects and activities as well as the use of field experiences beyond the traditional classroom. Block scheduling also offers a way to deal with larger than desired class sizes by creating a consistent source of coverage for students involved with the team. If a teacher needs to give all his/her attention to ten students on a particular day, taking them on a field experience or working with them in-house, then one of the other teachers can absorb the balance of students with the favor being returned when called on.

The physical proximity of team classrooms is desirable for several practical reasons. Proximity is nine-tenths of communication. Adjoining classrooms allow teachers to talk to each other, to monitor each other's rooms, and to share resources. Physical proximity is also a significant factor in creating program identity. Having a sense of place facilitates the development of a sense of purpose, unity and program culture. Holding students accountable for being where they are supposed to be becomes a much more natural process when all their classes, and also their lockers, are in a centralized location.

A common planning period for all team teachers is one of those seemingly little details that have huge consequences. Mutual planning can create a powerful vision and focus cooperative energy on producing the desired results. When a common planning period exists, it is natural to compare notes concerning how students are doing, to develop interdisciplinary curricula, to develop supportive relationships, to keep each other abreast of emerging difficulties and to plan collaboratively to address them. Conversely, when teachers do not have a common planning time these processes just do not happen to the same degree without much extra effort.

If teaming requires more commitment then is appropriate for your situation then there are less sweeping measures that can facilitate the integration of experiential methods in your classroom.

Some thoughts on teacher support

Being the champion of innovative programs and teaching ideas will often lead to Herculean work loads. Innovative teachers need support. But teachers do not often get support. This is why good teachers often burn out. It is easy to get carried away by our passions. While this is wonderful, it is important to keep one foot planted in the realities of taking care of ourselves. Pay attention to pacing, letting things change slowly. Seek some form of compensation for additional work loads and network with like-minded educators. Energy is well spent on building mechanisms to help

> **A common planning period for all team teachers is one of those seemingly little details that have huge consequences.**

avoid the sense of isolation and overwork which often surrounds championing new ideas in a school district.

Pace yourself. Commit to the long run. Countless innovative programs that had glorious and meteoric starts die with equal abruptness because of poor pacing and burnout. If the initiative for bringing Outward Bound into your schools is coming from the district level, helping them to set their sights on a slow pace of change is critical. Our district was fortunate to have the aggressive support of our superintendent as we worked to integrate Outward Bound into our schools. Our superintendent's vision and commitment paved an easy road for starting our programs, but the pace was too fast and it cost us dearly in the long run. The district's focus was on impacting hundreds of students right away, so we moved in this direction and neglected to develop an infrastructure through the training of teachers and administrators and the development of curriculum. When our budget was sharply reduced due to state-funding cutbacks, we were no longer able to subcontract out for the expertise we needed to run quality and safe programs, and we had not developed the internal resources required to sustain our effort. Our program was reduced to a vestigial remnant of the vision of its inception three years earlier. In retrospect I highly recommend that a minimum of a year be committed to professional development for teachers and administrators before students even enter the equation. This can be a tough sell to a school board, but it is a worthy fight and common sense is on your side. Outward Bound schools or the Association for Experiential Education should be able to point you toward professional development resources in your area.

If you are working from a grass roots level as an individual or as a small group of educators in attempting to bring Outward Bound and Outward Bound values to your school district, than the scale of the issues will be smaller, but the basic issues are the same. Seek quality professional development and go after curriculum development money to build a base of knowledge and materials. Develop several good units or programs and test them out. Strive for quality, not quantity, and build slowly.

Once your program is up and running, you may well find that you need to work with students during some evening and weekend time. Traditional schedules make the implementation of many experiential programs and teaching approaches difficult during the school day. You may also find yourself needing large amounts of time to write curricula, develop programs, or prepare grant proposals. If this describes your situation, consider asking for compensatory time or pay to support your efforts. Asking for compensation means that you care enough not to want to burn out. I know teachers who get the Monday off following all weekend trips they run while others draw extra salary. Using weekend and evening time is a great way to avoid the hassles of scheduling conflicts, but even when you are doing things you believe deeply in, it takes a toll. A commitment to a sustained program requires that you find ways to be compensated for your extra time. The teacher I know who gets Mondays off has been running an adventure-based leadership class, in which he uses weekend time, for fourteen years. If the district was not willing to make this small gesture of support then many students would have missed out on a very dynamic program. It is not too much to ask.

Communicate with like-minded educators. Access the community of teachers that believes in and can support what you are doing. Contact the Association for Experiential Education, in

Seek quality professional development and go after curriculum development money to build a base of knowledge and materials

Boulder, Colorado, or an Outward Bound School to find out what networks there are for teachers working on a similar path in your area. Take advantage of computer bulletin board services and electronic mail and use your computer as a networking and information sharing tool. Contacting the Association for Experiential Education or Outward Bound can get you leads for these services also. Tap into conference budgets and get to an Association for Experiential Education regional conference in your area. And, work internally to set up common planning periods or lunch groups with teachers and administrators who share your vision.

Some ideas for building support

Since this kind of program may be a new idea for the system or for the individual school and its staff, it would be wise to remember that human beings are often afraid of what they do not understand. Administrators and other teachers may experience anxiety and fear of the changes they see taking place in their schools. When people in institutional settings are afraid, they may work to sabotage the new project in quiet (or not so quiet) ways. When I was part of a team of teachers working on an experience-based learning project in a traditional public high school, I witnessed the continual harassment of our highly esteemed English teacher by her department head over the most vague and suspect of reasons. The issue was purely one of control: our classrooms did not look like what the department head was used to, and he felt that they were dangerous and should be put back into "order." Despite our English teacher's strong reputation in the district, it took several emotionally charged meetings with the building principal to save our teammate from having to attend weekly "teacher remediation" sessions. The benefit of this incident was that it drove us to recognize the value of public relations. The flagship of our public relations efforts was the distribution of a newspaper published by our students. This newsletter was sent to faculty, administration and the parents of our students and served us well. Students of all ages can create and publish newsletters that highlight their learning adventures. The distribution of our newsletter spawned numerous discussions concerning our program and our "unique" approach to learning. The newsletter was a forum for students to present what they had learned and how they had learned it. This forum could be used to highlight the successes of our program. One of my favorite pieces was a journalistic recounting of how it felt for a high school senior, who was consistently in serious conflict with the office, to be teaching the basic skills of rock climbing to the assistant principal who was in charge of disciplining him. The assistant principal's support was greatly enhanced from that moment on. The very existence of a student produced newsletter exemplified the active role students played in our classes. Along with being a public relations tool, the newsletter aided in motivation and helped to bring closure to learning activities. Although our students often griped about the work required to get the paper out, they were always very proud of the final product. They loved to see their work in print and knowing that others would be seeing it also created a beneficial tension and a sense of real consequence.

While we focused our attention on the newsletter, other forums through which students can share their projects with the school and local community are equally valid. Public access TV, for example, may be another means of exposing student work to an audience beyond the classroom.

Working with parents

The creative involvement of parents is one of the most powerful ways to build support and gain instructional benefits for your program. One way to structure the involvement of parents is to ask a parent from each classroom to develop a database of parental resources. This database can

> The creative involvement of parents is one of the most powerful ways to build support and gain instructional benefits for your program.

include areas of expertise, availability for chaperone duties, areas of special interest, etc. Once created, the database can be used throughout the year. When parents are involved in school activities, even in small ways, everyone benefits. You may find parents who are artists, mechanics, computer programmers, bakers, musicians, bird enthusiasts, or wood workers within your school community who will share their talents with your students. In the process they may become strong supporters of your style of education as well. You never know when this grassroots support may become critical (school committee funding decisions, etc.)

Other ways to involve parents include a seemingly simple, but often overlooked informational phone call. The signature trait of our program became the vast number of parent phone calls we would make every month. We called to ask parents to support us in working on certain behaviors, to set up parent conferences, to ask for their reinforcement of social or academic expectations, or to let them know when their son or daughter had a noteworthy success. For the most part parents thoroughly appreciated our persistence and consistency in keeping them informed. It helped with students also, for they knew that we would call home for both problems and successes. Over the course of most months the four teachers in our experience-based program would make more parent phone calls than the rest of the school combined. This statistic gained us great favor with the building administration. To support this calling effort, the administration allowed us to run a phone line into our classroom area and this made calling significantly more convenient.

Another mechanism for building the support of parents is to host a parent night built around a pot-luck supper and an appropriate speaker. An extension of this idea that we often talked about, but never implemented, was to host a weekend seminar for parents that would engage them in activities similar to those used with their children and allow for focus groups to address current educational and school management issues. The seminar would not have to attract a large number of parents to be a highly useful experience.

Working with the students

Enlist the investment of students
Classroom structure should say to a student "I see you as a full partner in this learning venture." Students often behave much as we expect them to and many students will respond with enthusiasm and accountability when they are exposed to a classroom atmosphere of trust and developmentally appropriate responsibility.

In an activity-based project, students are often asked to work in a self-directed and responsible manner and the teacher will often need to work with students individually or in small groups. For this approach to be successful the students need to demonstrate a high degree of independence, patience, and initiative. If they do not, the classroom can become chaotic. For this reason, attending to student motivation and investment is particularly important when using experience-based learning models. Fortunately, educational research suggests that experience-based learning models are potentially more effective at sparking the intrinsic motivation of students than more traditional didactic styles of teaching. One mechanism for tapping into this potential for student investment and motivation is to include students in the planning process and create elements of choice within the curriculum. When we are in a situation by choice, our investment in seeing it

---

Classroom structure should say to a student "I see you as a full partner in this learning venture."

through is enhanced. Structure choice in ways appropriate to your students' developmental level. Students can be involved in everything from choosing subject matter to determining performance standards.

Another important factor in nurturing student investment is the development of full and healthy classroom relationships. Relationships are built on shared experience, but in many classes students see only a small dimension of their teacher's and fellow classmates personalities. Often students do not even know each others' names. One fast way to build classroom relationships is to start off your classes with a high-impact adventurous experience. I have started my classes with ropes course days, hiking trips, rappels down rock faces, and sunset walks on a beach. The important element is that the experience encompass a sense of adventure and be focused on group activities. It is truly amazing how much impact these simple activities can have on the culture of a class. Students came to know some of their classmates in a light never before seen, and seeing that I, the teacher, was willing to spend "real world" time with them and provide them with exciting opportunities validated me in their eyes. These experiences also marked my classes as "different," and as this reputation grew among the student body, new students entering my classes grew to have a non-traditional set of classroom expectations.

Provide opportunities for students to develop the affective and social skills they need to succeed.
Students are often not comfortable working in non-traditional learning styles. The demands placed on students in an active project and in activity-based approaches to learning are very different from the demands placed on them in more traditional, teacher-centered approaches. When students do not know what is expected of them, or when they do not have the basic skills to meet those expectations, poor or misdirected behavior can often follow. Students need time and training to change expectations and habits that may be deeply ingrained, and they need training in the cognitive, affective, and social skills that will be demanded of them.

Affective and social skills are critical to a student's ability to succeed in school and life but traditionally very little time is spent training these dimensions of a student's development. There are very few classes that are specifically designed to address the affective and social dimensions of a student's growth and the individual, non-interactive role students are relegated to in many of their academic classes make these dimensions of a student's development inaccessible in these forums also. In contrast, the teachers who engage their students in an interactive experience-based approach to learning have a great opportunity to address affective and social issues as a natural part of the curriculum. When students are working in groups, a whole new dimension of the educational process becomes available. Each individual's interactions within the group, the roles they play, the contributions they make, their effectiveness in communication, their ability to assume leadership responsibilities or support others in that role, and their approaches to solving problems can all now be addressed. By concentrating on these affective and social issues you help the students to become more efficient in the process of learning, improve their skills in human interaction, and decrease classroom chaos.

The initiative problems presented in this book are especially effective training vehicles for affective and social skills. Initiatives impel students (and adults) to work cooperatively in group problem-solving exercises that are usually interesting, challenging, intense, and accomplishable. These exercises usually provide great fodder for a subsequent debrief concerning each

One fast way to build classroom relationships is to start off your classes with a high impact adventurous experience.

Implementation

individual's role in the group, their effectiveness in communication, the ability of the group to work together, and other affective and social skills. Videotaping your students during several of these initiatives can be a learning tool that is both riveting and riotous. Students love to watch themselves on tape.

As you work to cultivate an atmosphere of trust, independence, and compassion, you will often be fighting the general building culture. With hostility raging in the hallways and Pavlovian bells ringing every forty-five minutes it is easy for the external environment to impinge upon your classroom. While this is often deeply frustrating, these counterproductive dimensions of the school culture can be used as a learning opportunity. Be aware of the differences between what you are creating in your classroom and what exists in other facets of the school culture and use this contrast to help your students raise their awareness.

Some thoughts on transportation:
Teachers who wish to provide increased contact between students and the local community or teach through adventurous activities and projects will have to deal with the constraints of transportation. The use of learning environments other than the traditional classroom is an important component of involving the students with the community and maintaining a sense of adventure and intrigue. Unfortunately, transporting students takes time and money, two things which are often in short supply.

If you are not working in a teaming situation with block schedules, students will be missing other classes when you go on a field trip. Great attention to communicating the "who, when, and why" for each field experience will help diffuse the territorial wrath that can be raised by pulling students out of other classes.

One way to avoid this conflict is to use after-school time or weekends. It is virtually impossible to get all the students to attend a class trip at these times but if you creatively design these experiences to be optional, then the advantages are complete flexibility. Making use of non-school hours is also a perfect time to pilot school programs that might not be approved during regular school hours.

Sixteen passenger vans may require no special license in many states and are widely available as rentals. If participants are capped at fifteen students, then the whole class and the teacher can fit into one van, and driving time can be used for class activities. If more vehicles are needed for a field trip, it is a perfect opportunity to involve administrators, other teachers, and parents in your activities. Strong support can result from creating opportunities for first-hand involvement in your activities. On a caving trip for my geology class I solicited driving and supervision help from Greg, a social studies teacher in the building who had wanted to see what these "Outward Bound" trips were all about. While in the cave Greg led a small group, including several students in his classes, down a tight side passage. He had never been caving before, but he crawled through the mud, and squeezed through small rock openings with persistence and passion. After the trip Greg commented that his relationship with his students on the trip had fundamentally changed. There was now the bond of shared stressful experience and Greg felt that this personal contact translated directly into more productive classroom relationships. By asking for help our program gained much more than just a driver.

The use of learning environments other than the traditional classroom is an important component of involving the students with the community and maintaining a sense of adventure and intrigue.

One way to avoid the problems of transporting large numbers of students and pulling students out of other classes is to structure field experiences as "homework." Create long-term assignments which require students to do their internships or field work on their own time. These assignments require a large degree of independence and must be age-appropriate and highly structured if students are to succeed. The field sites that students choose must be easily accessible for them through consistently available means of transportation. Expectations and instructions at every stage of the assignment must be clearly understood and class time must be spent on processing and supporting their experiences. If the students' work includes any type of internship or work experience, there should be a designated supervisor at the site. The teacher can work with the supervisor to structure and support the students' experience.

Some thoughts on money.
How do you work with what you have and how do you get what you need? These are simple questions with no simple answers. Change often equals money. Initially seed money is required for the training of teachers and administrators, developing curricula, and acquiring support materials. When programs are up and running, some budget will be needed for additional materials, training, program evaluation, and transportation. These financial needs are no different for Outward Bound programs than they are for any other new initiative within a school district. All programs require seed money and some budget to support the normal operations.

One approach to getting the financial support you need is to use existing budgets to support your initiatives. Tap into training and workshop budgets, apply for summer curriculum development money, and ask for more control over the materials and supplies budget that already exists to support you as a teacher. You do not need a tremendous amount more money, you just might need to allocate your portion differently. For example, if you do not need to spend money on textbooks but instead need to buy other materials, it might be possible, with a supportive principal as your advocate, to get some of that line item apportioned to meet your real need. Ask for more control of the money that is already in place to support teaching staff.

Whatever seed money is available would be well spent on professional development for interested teachers and administrators. There is often great pressure to work immediately with students, but in the long run investing in the training of staff who have the skills to develop programs internally will

One approach to getting the financial support you need is to use existing budgets to support your initiatives. Tap into training and workshop budgets, apply for summer curriculum development money, and ask for more control over the materials and supplies budget that already exists to support you as a teacher.

be much more cost-effective then hiring adventure education sub-contractors to work with students.

You can work to keep costs down by concentrating on local resources. With creative programming you can often find ways to run quality learning adventures close to home. Two other key principles for cost control are "recycle and scrounge." Wonderful materials can be obtained with the aggressive application of these principles. One of the teachers in our team was a master of the form letter. He would identify needs, such as computer software, camping equipment or electronic parts, and draft a request letter. He would then canvas local businesses. These queries often met with surprising success, and we received items from backpacks to small computers to couches. Free materials can also be found at many museums. In our area, for example, the Science Museum collects recycled industrial products and provides them free of charge to teachers.

The database of parental resources can also be used to keep costs down. Parents may be able to provide services, such as printing, transportation, and guest lectures, free of charge.

Student fund-raising projects can also be structured as an integral part of the curriculum. One of the benefits of a project and activity approach to learning is that it facilitates the creation of marketable products, or the acquisition of "clients." With creativity these approaches can translate to increased student motivation, due to the sense of real consequence, and money to fund your program. If the students have played an integral role in funding an activity, trip, or purchase of materials, there is the benefit of increased investment.

Educational reform is currently a hot area for grant funding. There is an aura of mystery that surrounds the grant process, but teachers know better than anyone what they need to effect positive change. The process of writing a grant proposal can be a great mechanism for bringing a group of teachers together and forcing the clear articulation of your vision. On the practical level, as countless school districts are being forced to cut back programs and teachers to subsistence levels due to budget constraints, the pursuit of private sector and foundation grant money is increasingly becoming the only option for funding creative new programs. The good news is that grant money is out there for educational reform programs. *Education Week* and *Teacher* magazines publish listings of current grant possibilities. For smaller grants local businesses and community organizations are the logical places to start.

If you decide to pursue grant money as part of your funding strategy then you would be well advised to research your district administration's receptivity and ability to support your vision. The team of teachers I worked with learned the hard way what can happen if this step is not aggressively pursued. Due to our district's across-the-board cut of all non-state-mandated programs, our $50 thousand budget was cut to zero. In response to this we pursued grant money. We convened a group of interested teachers from throughout the district and designed a proposal based on the model of our existing experience-based school-within-a-school program. Several conceptual changes to our program were agreed upon to meet the requirements of the grant we were focusing on but the heart of the program remained the same. After a draft of the grant was submitted, we were told by the sponsoring company that we were on the right track and things looked good for a $1 million commitment over the next five years. At that point we received a

> **On the practical level, as countless school districts are being forced to cut back programs and teachers to subsistence levels due to budget constraints, the pursuit of private sector and foundation grant money is increasingly becoming the only option for funding creative new programs.**

letter from our superintendent which stated that we had done "great work" and that one of the assistant superintendents would take over the grant proposal from here. Far from being a supportive gesture, this stripped us from our work and left us fighting a losing battle for control over the substance of the grant. The final grant proposal was drafted under secretive circumstances and further dialogue was aggressively blocked by the central administration. The district did receive the grant, $1 million. Unfortunately, the heart of the program, such as the purchase of a van and computers, the hiring of a coordinator to head the evaluation of the program, and the pursuit of continued funding, were sacrificed to large line items added to pay the salary of district administrators whose jobs were on the line due to budget cuts.

Work with the administration from the very start of the grant process. The dialogue concerning how to target the grant needs to be agreed upon in the early stages of the process. The first step is a clear and common vision, and leadership in this process will often need to come from the teachers.

Implementation

OUTWARD BOUND'S APPROACH TO TEACHING AND LEARNING

Initiatives are activities that present problems or challenges to a group or individual that do not have a right or wrong answer. The tasks are designed to challenge the physical and mental abilities of the group's participants. Some initiatives require apparatus, special props and/or special settings, others do not, and in a school setting they can provide everyone with an opportunity to deal with and learn from their own behaviors and the behavior of others.

The skills and qualities practiced include persevering, cooperating, compassion, listening, supporting, expressing, creating, negotiating, risk-taking, leading, trusting, planning, and teamwork. Initiatives are excellent brief examples of learning by doing. The group process helps the learner discover that some achievements are beyond individual capacity, but well within the supportive capacity of the group, and that the group's successes are shared by all its members.

In using initiatives as learning tools, first present simple, less complex tasks and then advance to more complex and difficult tasks. Debriefing the behaviors and observations adds to the learning process and gives the feedback necessary to apply the learning to future activities.

Chapter 4 presents an overview of processes and concepts to enhance the efficacy of initiatives. Chapters 5, 6, and 7 present initiatives, submitted by past and present Outward Bound staff, that were selected for adaptability to indoor and outdoor school environments and their ease of use.

Photo left: The discipline of attentiveness to detail, reliance on others and communication skills learned while participating in outdoor activities is easily transferred to the classroom.

Initiatives

CHAPTER 4

Initiatives

*A mind that is stretched by a new experience
can never go back to its old dimensions.*

— Oliver Wendell Holmes

Two sets of experiences happen simultaneously in an initiative. The first has to do with what is going on in the mind of each participant. The second concerns what is happening with the group as a whole — the group's "collective mind." Though initiatives can be done simply for enjoyment, they are powerful tools that can be used to activate the Learning Cycle (page 20) and establish the context for learning (page 24).

The Individual's Experience

Initiatives help us think about how we react when confronted with challenging situations. Do we experience fear, anxiety, or pleasure? How do we react when we get frustrated? Are we willing to be leaders in certain circumstances and not in others? Do we have doubts about our abilities, especially when performing tasks in front of others? How exactly do we work with others? What barriers do we have that might prevent us from being part of the group? Every initiative elicits a different set of questions from each member of the group. One person may be enthusiastic about solving a mental problem like the "toxic waste" initiative, but frozen with fear when it comes time for the "trust-fall" sequence. Each initiative brings out different feelings in each participant. But all of them provide opportunities for individuals to look carefully at themselves and how they behave.

The Group's Experience

While all these thoughts and feelings are going on inside each of the participants, they also belong to a group. The group is much more than just the sum of each member's experiences. The group has a life of its own. It is a collection of interdependent individuals: people who come together to achieve a mutual purpose.

Encouraging a group to work effectively is a complicated business. It has three core tasks:

1. Accomplishing its goals;
2. Working at fostering and strengthening relationships among group members; and
3. Developing and changing in ways that improve its effectiveness. [1]

Special thanks to Denis Udall, Expeditionary Learning Outward Bound and Jon Howard, Hurricane Island Outward Bound School for contributing to this chapter.

Initiatives

1. Johnson and Johnson, <u>Joining Together and Alone Group Therapy and Group Skills</u>, Prentice Hall, Inc. Englewood Cliffs, New Jersey.

Choosing and Presenting an Initiative

There are five important points to keep in mind when presenting an initiative.[2]

1. What's your goal?

You should have a clear idea why you are introducing an initiative. Consider what it is you want to accomplish. For instance, you might ask, "What difficulties is the group having and how can a particular initiative help it work together more effectively?" Initiative games are, generally, a means to an end, not ends in themselves. Some of the initiatives are more game-like than others. It's okay to introduce a game purely for the fun of it, but even then you should have a clear goal in mind. Each one is designed to develop a set of group skills. It's best to think about your group's needs and then select an initiative tailored to those needs.

2. Selecting an appropriate activity.

Choose an activity suited to the ability of your group. Asking a group to undertake a task which is beyond its ability is setting it up for failure, though it is normal for a group to experience setbacks and frustration as it toils away on a task. Don't let this scare you away from introducing a challenging activity.

3. Presenting an initiative.

Tell the group all the rules, procedures and safety considerations before beginning the activity. Then step back and allow the group to go to it. Don't intervene unless someone's safety is compromised. Often groups will dive into solving a problem without really having developed a plan of action. Some members might act on one idea while others stand around discussing yet another. You might see scant evidence of communication and cooperation. At such times, it's tempting to stop the activity and point out what is happening. This may be appropriate in some situations, but often it's best to let the group continue on its own for a while. The timing of such interventions is crucial. It may be important for the group to experience some initial failure and frustration before it's ready to consider other ways of working together.

4. How much time is enough?

There are at least two schools of thought about how much time to allow a group to accomplish an initiative. One approach is to let the group keep trying until it has finished the task. Remember, an initiative should be chosen with the particular group in mind. It should be challenging, but it should also be doable. Your group should be able to complete the initiative given adequate time and tenacity. Once in a while, you'll find that considerable time has lapsed and the group hasn't made any progress. You may begin to think they just won't be able to get it. Maybe you miscalculated the group's abilities or perhaps you selected the wrong initiative. In either case, this might be the right time for the second approach. Stop the group and either simplify the initiative or let the group break a rule long enough to make some headway. You might also want to come back to the task at another time.

5. Establishing A Supportive Environment.

Reflection is key to creating powerful, meaningful learning experiences, but it's not enough. We also need to build an environment where people feel safe enough to share their thoughts and feelings with one another. Both reflection and support are equally important aspects of processing;

> **The group is much more than just the sum of each member's experiences. The group has a life of its own.**

2. Benjy Simpson, Initiative Games, Butler County Community College, Butler, Pennsylvania, 1975.

they're like two sides of a coin. They need one another to make an integrated learning experience. Would we want to reflect deeply in the presence of others about why a particular experience had such a profound impact if we didn't feel respected and cared for? Probably not. If we're not supported emotionally by others, would we necessarily choose to think about our experiences? Probably not.

Facilitation

There are factors to consider when facilitating a group.[3]

Choose one person to facilitate
Group meetings work best when one person is charged with the responsibility to keep things moving along, such as keeping time, reminding people how to listen and thinking about how the group is working.

Open and close on a positive note
It is always good to close or open the sharing with appreciations of each other. This always brings smiles, laughs and relaxation to the sharing.

Keep in touch with your feelings
Where is your energy? Don't try to facilitate a processing session if you are distraught over a personal issue. You should resolve that issue first.

Set the tone
The leader's attitude will set the tone for the group. As a facilitator, you should be alert, centered, show positive energy, and keep your attention within the group.

Draw people out
Help others to clarify and articulate their feelings, thoughts, ideas and values. Ask questions. It is often helpful for someone to hear you repeat in a different way what they have said. It tells them you are listening and understanding.

Be aware of your physical surroundings
Make certain you are in a place where the group will be comfortable debriefing for an hour or more.

Timing
It's a good idea to conduct debriefing meetings immediately after major events and powerful experiences. Don't put it off even for a few hours. Much of the content and feelings will dissipate. Plan the time to do it.

Processing

There are two parts to processing a group's experience. The first involves reflection on the experience. The second has to do with establishing a supportive environment.

> Remember, an initiative should be chosen with the particular group in mind. It should be challenging, but it should also be doable.

Initiatives

3. Hawaii Bound School, <u>Hawaii Bound's Instruction Manual</u>, Honolulu, Hawaii 1980

Reflecting on Experience

Think about the variety of experiences you have every day. Many are commonplace. Others are exceptional or unusual. We can't possibly examine every aspect of our daily experiences — we have to make some choices—but it's important we take time out to look at ourselves, our actions and the influences in our lives.

The Experience-based Learning Cycle

The cycle begins with a concrete experience. At some point during or after the experience, we consider its importance and meaning. In the process of examining the experience, we abstract special lessons and concepts. Next, we remove those lessons from the contexts where we first learned them and apply them to new situations and new experiences. Then we ask ourselves, "What happened this time around? Did something change? If so, what?"

One phase leads to the next. If we leave out a phase, we won't get to the others. If we don't stop and reflect on our experiences, we won't learn from them. If we don't take the risk of applying lessons learned in new settings, then we are not using past experiences to guide future actions.

A Processing Tool

Here are three questions that can help you to structure reflection within a group:

> **"What?"**
> > **"So what?"**
> > > **"Now what?"**

The **"What"** pertains to the experience and how it affected the group's interaction. What did each of us experience? How did we feel? How did we respond? Who did what? How were decisions made? There are questions you can you ask to get the conversation going; they should be aimed at encouraging the group to tell its story of what occurred.

The **"So what"** concerns the meanings the group gives to a particular experience. What are the lessons we take away from this experience?

The **"Now what"** asks how the experience may be acted upon. What did we learn and how can this help us choose the best alternatives and reapply them to other situations? Since we have a good idea of what actually happened and what it meant to us, what do we do now?

Group Development [4]

Group theorists and social psychologists have developed models that try to capture the different phases groups move through in their development. Many of these models describe at least six stages of development:

Forming/Orientation
Norming
Storming/Dissatisfaction
Resolving
Performing/Production
Termination

Here's a description of each stage:

Stage One – Forming/Orientation Characteristics:
> Feeling moderately eager with high expectations.
> Feeling some anxiety: Where do I fit? What is expected of me?
> Testing the situation and leader figures.
> Depending on authority and hierarchy.
> Needing to find a place and establish oneself.

Stage Two – Norming Characteristics:
> Establishing group identity.
> Looking for rules and norms of behavior.
> Establishing roles.
> Establishing individual vs. group responsibility.
> Testing, experimenting. Power struggles.
> Focusing on leader. Group leaders beginning to emerge.
> Experiencing conflict but not openly confronted.
> Reluctant to commit to an action plan.

Stage Three – Storming/Dissatisfaction Characteristics:
> Experiencing a discrepancy between hopes and reality.
> Feeling dissatisfied with dependence on authority.
> Feeling frustrated and angry about goals, tasks and action plans.
> Reacting negatively toward leaders and other members.
> Competition for power and/or attention.

Stage Four – Resolving Characteristics:
> Decreasing dissatisfaction.
> Resolving discrepancies between expectations and reality.
> Resolving polarities and animosities.
> Developing harmony, trust, support and respect.
> Opening up and giving more feedback.
> Sharing responsibility and control.

(4) Tuckman, B.W. "Development sequence in small groups," Psychological Bulletin, 63 (1965), pp. 384-399.

Initiatives

Stage Five – Performing/Production Characteristics:

Feeling good about participating in team activities.
Working collaboratively and interdependently in whole and subgroups.
Feeling team strength.
Showing high confidence in accomplishing tasks.
Sharing leadership.
Feeling positive about success with tasks.
Performing at high levels.

Stage Six – Termination Characteristics:

Feelings of loss, nostalgia, as well as success and:
Accomplishment.
Fearing separation.
Loss of productivity.
Denying.
Floundering as a group.
Experiencing both positive and negative emotion.

The central idea behind this conceptual model is that, with adequate time and support, every group will move through these six stages. However, each will have its own pace; no two groups will pass through the six stages in exactly the same way or within the same time frame. Groups may also move back and forth between stages.

A group leader can use this model to understand important issues confronting the group at a particular juncture in its development. Understanding where a group is in its evolution is important. It allows us to see how we can structure activities and discussions that will move the group forward. Be wary of molding the group to fit the model. Look closely at the behavior and characteristics of your groups to see whether and where they are defined and illustrated by the theory.

Activities

There are many initiative activities that can be incorporated into the school curriculum. The activities presented in this book were submitted by present and past Outward Bound staff. They are divided into three categories according to the purposes for which they have been most often and successfully used: Social Connections; Developing Awareness and Promoting Group Problem-Solving Skills.

The activities you will find in chapters five through seven were selected for their ease of presentation, their modest time requirements and their adaptability to both indoor and outdoor environments. The format used to present each activity is based on the following outline:

Contributed By — The name of the Outward Bound staff member who submitted the activity and the school they represent. The contributor is not necessarily the creator of the activity.

What's Learned — Delineates the principal learnings that occur from participating in the activity.

Equipment — The props or materials needed to accomplish the activity.

Pre–activity Preparation — A description of what is required by the teacher when preparing to present the activity. (Not all required pre-activity preparation)

Overview — A general description of the activity including benefits and information helpful in using the activity.

Activity Introduction — A suggested approach to introducing the activity use a hypothetical story, a specific question to be answered, or a set of instructions to be used prior to engaging in the activity.

Description — A detailed explanation of the activity. In addition, some activities have variations that can be incorporated.

Solution — The most common way (but not the only way) to solve the problem or complete the task within the rules.

Rules, Safety, Special Considerations — Specific information that helps to ensure that the activity is done according to the generally accepted guidelines and safety procedures.

Debriefing Questions — Questions that could be asked as you discuss what happened during the activity.

Classroom Applications — a specific subject that the activity could be integrated with; skills and classroom behaviors that could be learned through participation.

Initiatives

CHAPTER 5

Social Connection Initiatives

In this category, participants are required to interact socially with others. These activities are generally used as icebreakers and presented as play. They place participants in situations where, through games, physical contact and the sharing of personal stories and experiences, the group members get to know each other.

Social Connections

Quick Reference Chart

Acitvity Name	What's Learned	Indoor or Outdoor	Minimum No. of Participants	Special Equipment Required	Pre-Activity Preparation Required	Classroom Application
Turbo to Warp Speed	Curiosity Expressiveness Creative Thinking Support	Either	5	Yes	No	Memorization skills and Sequencing data
Human Machine	Cooperation Trust	Either	5	No	No	Creativity Classroom relationships
Body Pass	Trust Risk–Taking	Either Either	5	No	Yes	Building classroom relationships
Artist Clay Model	Expressiveness Trust	Either	3	Yes	No	Art Creativity
Tiny Teach	Communications Self-confidence Risk-Taking Expressiveness	Either	3	No	No	Cooperative learning and peer teaching Inter-disciplinary
Three-Way Pull	Cooperation Communication	Either	9	Yes	Yes	Planning & Cooperation

Social Connections

Quick Reference Chart

Acitvity Name	What's Learned	Indoor or Outdoor	Minimum No. of Participants	Special Equipment Required	Pre-Activity Preparation Required	Classroom Application
Trolley	Communication Skills Teamwork Perseverance	Either	5	Yes	Yes	Organization skills Group cohesiveness
Group Munch	Trust Teamwork Communication	Either	5	Yes	Yes	Building classroom relationships
Heirlooms	Self-Confidence Risk–Taking Curiosity Expressiveness	Either Either	3	No	No	Oral presentation Multicultural
Home Sweet Home	Expressiveness Trust Self-Confidence	Either	3	Yes	No	Building classroom relationships
Gordion Knot	Communication Leadership Trust	Either	5	No	No	Building classroom relationships
Broken Squares	Problem-Solving Cooperation Communication	Either	5	Yes	Yes	Mathematics Creative thinking
Monster Race	Decision making Cooperation Trust	Outdoors	2 Groups of more than 12	No	No	Fun

Initiatives

Teaching Notes:

Group Juggle to Warp Speed

Contributed by: Mitchell Sakofs, Outward Bound Inc.

Creator: Project Adventure

What's learned
- Communication
- Creative thinking
- Expressiveness
- Support

Equipment
One or more items to juggle. (Example: tennis balls, oranges, koosh, balled-up socks, rubber snakes, large rubber insects, miniature footballs, or anything that is soft and can be juggled.) The objects used should vary in size and weight.

Pre-Activity Preparation
None required

Overview
This is a good icebreaker activity for groups from 5 to 20. It is an excellent name game and can be used to help people share their expectations or goals. Be aware of the size of the group, and give them plenty

Teaching Notes:

of room to move around. Encourage gentle, underhand tosses when throwing the object to be juggled.

Activity Introduction
Tell the group you would like to provide an opportunity for everyone to get to know each other better.

Description
Circle Up and explain that you would like everyone to introduce him or herself. Show them the item you will be passing around and explain that each person will be given an opportunity to introduce themselves when they have the item in their possession. The leader should start and provide an example of what to do. She may, for example, say her name and what she hopes to get out of the meeting. She should then toss the object across the circle to someone else. The person who catches the object should introduce themselves and in turn toss it to someone else. This pattern should be repeated until everyone has introduced themselves. Each person needs to remember from whom they received

the item and to whom they threw the item. Once the group has completed the task with one object, the teacher should challenge the group with a time trial to see how fast they can move the item through the sequence. Let the group go through the sequence once and then time it. A typical group, consisting of approximately 12 to 15 people will, at first, get the item through the sequence in about 15 +/– seconds. Challenge them to do it faster and faster.

Solutions
Most groups will assume that because they have to move the object through the sequence they must remain in the same position. But if the directions say "Everyone has to touch the ball in the same sequence," one solution to accelerate the movement of the object would be for people to reorganize themselves to increase efficiency. Some groups lineup in the order in which they touched the item, and have the first person hold it and run past everyone else, giving each person a chance to touch it. Other groups may

form a tight circle around the item and then quickly, and in sequence, simply touch it. Both solutions are fine, and in fact, any solution that get's people thinking and working together is fine.

Variations
During the initial passing of the item, you may ask them to:

• Say their names and what they would like to get out of the class.
• Say Thank You to the person throwing them the item and then say the name of the person to whom they will throw it after receiving the item, "Thank you, Tracy. My name is John." (and after finding out someone's name) "Catch, Zachary." Each student should give additional information beyond their names, e.g., "My name is Brian and I love sports," or "My name is Brian but my friends call me 'Briney.'"

Debriefing Questions
• How were ideas communicated?

• Were all ideas listened to? If not, what prevented listening from occurring?
• What did you do as a group to accomplish this task?
• Did you think that you'd have been able to do this so quickly at the first challenge? Why? Why not?
• What helped you as a group to achieve what you did?
• Were there any assumptions made about the directions or the objectives?
• Are there times when you had to "juggle" more then one task at a time? If so, how did you handle it?
• How can we communicate our ideas in other areas of school?
• How can we support each other's "juggling"?

Classroom Application
• Memorization skills and sequencing data
• Getting members of a class or group quickly acquainted with each other's names.

Initiatives

Human Machine

Contributed by: Phil Costello, Founder and Director of Project U.S.E.

What's Learned
• Cooperation
• Trust

Equipment
• None required

Pre-activity Preparation
• None required

Overview
This is a fun activity that can get the group laughing. It can help raise the level of awareness of personal boundaries and creates an opportunity for group interaction.

Activity Introduction
Our group is stranded on a vast deserted plain. We do not have enough food and water to walk out of this wasteland. But if we pull together and create a machine that will allow the group to utilize individual resources as various

machine parts, we can create a vehicle to rescue us.

Description
The group forms a large circle. One person goes to the center of the circle and moves and makes sounds to represent a machine part. Then a second person joins the first person in the center and attaches himself to the machine making a new movement and sound. The machine is complete when all members are in the

center and the entire machine is operating. Once the machine is operating it picks up speed and operates as fast as it can without breaking down.

Variations
The machine has to be of the nature to represent a specific industrial period in our history for example: steam engines, gasoline engines, a machine, or a moving piece of art.

Debriefing Questions
• How did it feel to attach yourself to another person in the group?
• Was there a specific reason why you chose that person?
• What was fun about this activity?
• How well did your group work together?

Classroom Application
• Creativity
• Creating a supportive classroom environment.

Teaching Notes:

Body Pass

Contributed by:
Tina Clark, Hurricane Island
Outward Bound School

Creator – New Games
Foundation, San Francisco,
Calif.

What's Learned
• Trust
• Risk-taking

Equipment
• None required

Pre-activity Preparation
• None required

Overview
Present this activity in an area free of hazardous obstacles like large boulders, desks, uneven terrain. This activity is an excellent icebreaker, but may require a little coaxing and coaching by the instructor. It is best to present the activity in a humorous manner. Keep it light and somewhat matter-of-fact. *Spotting is required and should be reviewed by all participants before the activity starts.*

Activity Introduction
Select an area that represents the distance equal to the group sitting down lined up in a straight line.

The head of the group is point A, the end of the group is point B. Ask the group this question, "Do you think we can pass each member of the group from point A to point B without the person who is being passed touching the ground?"

Description
Have all the participants sit on the ground, one in front

of the other, with legs spread out in front. Participants should sit as close as possible. The first member stands, crosses her arms across her chest, leans backward and is passed over the heads of the group. Each member is passed until all participants have returned to their original place.

Rules
The person being passed should keep her body as rigid as possible with arms crossed over her chest. She should be face up.

Safety
Two spotters should place themselves on either side of the line and accompany the individual being passed down the entire length of the line. The spotters need to assist the individual with the dismount. Touching is required in this activity. Teachers should assess the appropriateness of the activity for the group.

Debriefing Questions
• How did it feel to be passed over the head of each group member?
• Did you feel secure?
• What made you feel secure? Did it feel like you were taking a risk?
• What could have been done to make you feel more secure?
• Did the group work as a team to accomplish this task?
• What obstacles did the group have to overcome to complete the task?

Classroom Application
• Creating a supportive-classroom atmosphere.

Initiatives

Teaching Notes:

Artist Clay Model

Contributed By:
Charles Reade, Hurricane Island Outward Bound School

Creator – Project Adventure, Hamilton, Mass.

What's Learned
- Trust
- Expressiveness
- Risk-taking

Equipment
- Blindfolds (One per group of three individuals)

Pre-activity Preparation
- None required

Overview
This is a fun, light activity designed to get members of a group to feel comfortable with each other.

Activity Introduction
You are a great blind sculptor. You must use skills other then sight to recreate the figure before you using human clay.

Description
Divide the group into smaller groups of 3 participants each and give the following directions:

Group member No.1 is blindfolded and is the artist . Member No. 2 assumes a distinct position and is the model. Member No. 3 is the clay. The blindfolded artist must mold (member No. 3) the clay into the same position assumed by the model (member No. 2). Each member of the group takes a turn as the artist, model and clay. Once the model assumes the position to be molded, there is no talking or other form of communication.

Special Considerations
Because this activity requires touching, teachers should assess the appropriateness of the activity for the group, and be aware that inappropriate touching can be an issue. The teacher should make clear to the group what is appropriate touching. The teacher should monitor the activity to ensure emotional safety. (An option is to use real clay to avoid the issue of touching.)

Debriefing Questions
- What did it feel like to be the artist, model and clay?
- What difficulties did you experience in recreating the model?
- What senses/skills were used to complete the activity?

Classroom Application
- Art
- Sensory Awareness
- Creativity

Teaching Notes:

Tiny Teach

Contributed by:
Gruffie Clough, Colorado
Outward Bound School

What's Learned
• Teamwork
• Communications
• Self-confidence
• Risk-taking
• Expressiveness

Equipment
• None required

Pre-activity Preparation
• None required

Overview
This activity provides opportunities for all participants to become teachers and learners; it also demonstrates that everyone has something of value to share, and thus highlights the value of each member of the class.

This is a good activity to start with at the beginning of a school year, and it can be extended into many different subject areas.

Activity Introduction
In this activity, each member of the class is going to have

the opportunity to teach other class members something he/she knows very well.

Description
The individual participants organize into groups of two or three. Encourage participants to join with people they don't know. In each small group, one participant becomes an A. The other is B. The A member selects something to teach B in two or three minutes. For example:

a song
a poem
a phrase in a different language
a dance step
a riddle
the name of a flower
how to braid hair
etc.

When time is up, the group comes back together and the Bs are asked to tell or demonstrate to the group what they learned. When everyone who wants to has talked, have the dyads meet again and reverse roles.

Special Considerations
Insure all efforts to demonstrate a new skill are applauded. If someone is having difficulty coming up with an activity, the facilitator should help her along. The facilitator may want to review some of the skills being taught to determine their appropriateness. The facilitator should be prepared to break students into groups, especially if the activity is done at the beginning the school year.

Debriefing Questions
• How, when, and where might you use what you have learned?
• How did it feel to be the teacher?
• How did it feel to be the learner?
• Why did you teach the skill you did?
• What did you learn about teaching?

Classroom Application
• Cooperative Learning and peer teaching

Initiatives

Teaching Notes:

Three-Way Pull

*Contributed by: Jake Jagel,
Thompson Island Outward
Bound Education Center*

*Creator – Project Adventure,
Hamilton, Mass.*

What's Learned
• Cooperation
• Communications
• Teamwork

Equipment
• 1″ Manila rope - three
  50′ lengths
• A rag or other flag
  material

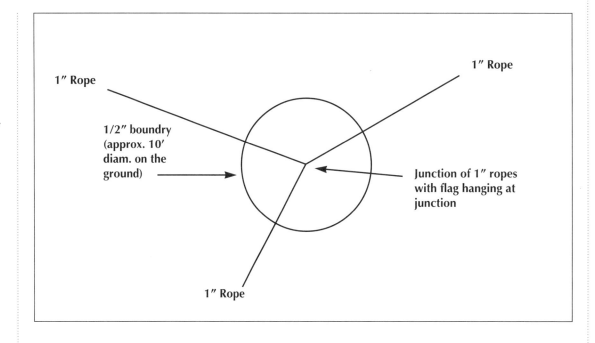

Pre-activity Preparation
Tie the three 1″ ropes together and set the 1/2″ rope as a boundary circle. Tie the flag at the junction of the three ropes..

The Three-Way Pull is a good example of an activity in which the group perceives a solution and discovers its limitations as it grasps the value of alternative solutions.

Activity Introduction
In 1050 A.D. three great armies set out to retrieve the holy ring from the circle of evil. (Each group represents one army) To obtain the ring, an army or armies has to pull the ring to its boundary line.

Description
The larger group is divided into three equal smaller teams of equal size and similar physical size. The task is for one group to pull the flag as quickly and efficiently as possible to one side without stepping inside the circle. At the signal each team starts to pull. If a group member is pulled into the circle the activity starts over.

Rules
• Do not allow group members to wrap the rope around themselves.
• The group should be standing with rope in hand ready to pull before the signal is given.

Debriefing Questions
• What went on?
• What was the task?

• How did the group define the three sides and why?
• What's the difference between cooperation and competition? What are some examples?
• How did each small group communicate with the other?

Classroom Application
• Cooperation vs. competition in the classroom
• Teamwork in class activities

62

Teaching Notes:

Trolley

Contributed by: Peter Bailey, Voyageur Outward Bound School

Creator – Project Adventure, Hamilton, Mass.

What's Learned
- Teamwork
- Communication
- Perseverance

Equipment
- Four 12' 2"x4" boards
- 30 feet of 1/2" manila rope

Pre-activity Preparation
The construction of the trolley requires time, woodworking tools and skills. (See diagram)

Overview
If a group is having difficulty working together, this activity should help the members sort out the issues. The excercise requires a very high level of teamwork.

Activity Introduction
The object of this activity is to move the entire group

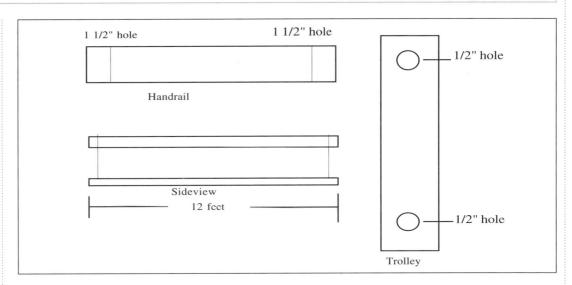

1 1/2" hole   1 1/2" hole

Handrail

Sideview

12 feet

1/2" hole

1/2" hole

Trolley

from point A to point B. In the space between points A and B is a pit of boiling oil and only the trolleys can get the group across.

Description
Standing on the tops of the two trolleys, the group must move from point A to point B, a distance of about 25 to 30 feet. Allow the group a certain amount of time to come up with a solution. If any member of the group touches the ground, the group has to return to point A and start again. After the group masters the basic skill of walking, put some obstacles in the path from point A

to point B. Have the group return to point A using a different strategy.

Variation – Blind/Mute Trolley
All but two members of the group are blindfolded. These two sighted participants, however, must participate in the activity without speaking. Explain the activity to the sighted, mute participants. Their job then becomes communicating the activity to those who are blindfolded. If a participant steps or falls off the trolley, the entire group must return to the starting point.

Debriefing Questions
- What were some of the things you experienced in getting the group to work together?
- How did the group resolve working as a team?
- How did the group communicate? What did you learn about communications?
- How did you feel when blindfolded?
- How did it feel to be mute?
- What made the activity successful?

Classroom Application
- Organizational Skills and Group Cohesiveness

Initiatives

Teaching Notes:

Group Munch

Contributed by: Kelly Gregg, Voyageur Outward Bound School

What's Learned
• Compassion
• Perseverance
• Trust
• Teamwork
• Communication

Equipment
• One bandanna per group member
• Lunch for the group, i.e., crackers, peanut butter, jelly, fruit, vegetables, bread, etc.
• Eating utensils (if required)
• A ground cover (if necessary)

Pre-Activity Preparation
Cover the lunch site with the ground cloth and do what is necessary to prepare the food.

Overview
Group Munch is a good activity to use midday, after a series of initiatives. It can sustain the energy of a group and extend learning.

Activity Introduction
As a result of a rare and special virus, each group member has lost her ability to use her right or left arm. In the middle of the group are the ingredients needed to develop a vaccine to cure this rare virus. The group, as a whole, must prepare and feed the other group members so they can be cured.

Description
Circle up and using bandannas tie everyone together, right hand to left hand. The object is to prepare the food and eat.

Variation-Reliance Munch
Prior to serving the meal, write handicapping conditions on index cards; one condition per card, e.g.,

blind, quadriplegic, no arms, deaf, mute, etc. Then, just before the meal, circle up and explain to your students that you will soon be handing them a card and they are to role-play what's on the card. Hand out the cards and start the meal.

Rules
Everyone must stay connected while eating.

Debriefing Questions
• Did they like their lunch?
• How did the process of feeding others work?
• Were there any give-and-take experiences? What were they?
• How were individual needs met?
• Did you see any situations when you were rewarded?
• What similar experiences have you had that relate to this initiative?

Classroom Application
• Classroom relationship building

Social Connection Initiative

Heirlooms: Family, Community, Personal

Contributed by: Huck Truitt, Colorado Outward Bound School

Creator – Ann Juramillo and Ed Aguilor

What's Learned
• Trust
• Self-confidence
• Self-esteem
• Self-concept
• Risk-taking
• Expressiveness

Equipment
• none required (Optional: clay, crayons, markers, pictures)

Pre-activity Preparation
• none required

Overview
This activity requires a quiet environment, free from distractions. The group experience provides students with an opportunity to learn about each other, their

respective backgrounds, cultures, ethnicity, religions, values, and communities.

Activity Introduction
Our possessions are a clear representation of our values and who we are.

Description
Students are asked to bring to the group an object representative of who they are

and where they come from. Each student presents and describes his "heirloom" to the group. Members in the group may ask questions after each student describes his heirloom to the group.

Special Consideration
It is important for the instructor to be aware of individual emotions and monitor the group's behavior.

Debriefing Questions
What have you learned about each other and the group by doing this activity? Was there anything that surprised you?
Were any of your assumptions or perceptions about other group members confirmed, or have they changed?

Classroom Application
• Oral classroom presentations
• Exploring roots
• Going beyond first impressions

Teaching Notes:

Home Sweet Home

Contributed by: Mitch Sakofs, Outward Bound Inc.

What's Learned
- Expressiveness
- Trust
- Self-confidence

Equipment
- Crayons, markers, poster paper, magazine pictures, newsprint.

Pre-Activity Preparation
- none required

Overview
This activity is an effective way to accelerate the process of your class members getting to know each other.

Activity Introduction
The students will be given paper and assorted drawing materials and asked to draw a picture of their homes. Tell them they can draw a picture of the home they currently live in or a home that they remember fondly. As they begin their pictures,

they should also be encouraged to draw any and all details that seem relevant. They might want to place the home in a neighborhood, show cars, trees and other elements of where they grew up. Though they should be encouraged to make their drawings as accurate as possible, indicate that they will be given an opportunity to share their drawings with the rest of the class, and give an oral tour.

Description
Give everyone about 15 to 20 minutes to complete their drawings. Once completed, circle up and one-by-one ask students to show the class their drawings and talk about them. Encourage them to go beyond a physical description, and share memories of events or feelings that may surface as they describe their homes. Allow them between five and 10

minutes of uninterrupted time to talk, and then allow approximately five minutes for questions.

Debriefing Questions
The debriefing is incorporated into the presentation of each individual's drawing.

Classroom Application
- Classroom relationship building

Teaching Notes:

Human Knot

Contributed by: Charles Reade, Hurricane Island Outward Bound School

What's Learned
• Communication
• Leadership
• Cooperation

Equipment
• None required

Pre-activity Preparation
• None

Overview
This an excellent lead-up activity to other activities that require touching and physical support. Participation requires very close contact and cooperation with other group members.

Activity Introduction
Circle-up and have each group member put his right arm into the circle and take hold of someone else's hand. Repeat the same with the left hand, connecting with someone else's left hand, creating a tangled human knot. Conduct an energy squeeze to ensure

everyone is connected properly.

Description
The objective is to untangle the knot to its most simple form—usually one circle or perhaps two interlocking circles. Group members may shift the position of their hands, but they may not let go. If the group finds itself in a particularly difficult bind, one option available is to strategically allow one of the bonds to be briefly broken to help the group along. This last step requires judgment on the part of the leaders, for there are times when you may not want to help a group get through a difficult and seemingly unresolvable problem. There are, of course, other times when it is more appropriate to offer this type of assistance.

Special Consideration
Because students will find themselves extremely close to each other and touching, assess the appropriateness of this activity for your students.

Debriefing Questions
• What were the keys to success?
• How was a solution achieved?
• Was there a leader or leaders?
• How were they chosen?
• What qualities did the leaders have?
• Once you, individually, were untangled, what did you do? (stay involved, check out, etc.)
• How did the physical layout of the task affect communication? How did communication occur?
• Identify a knot in your life where using what you've learned here would help to untangle it.
• What do you need to untangle that knot?

Classroom Application
• Classroom relationship building
• Creative thinking

Initiatives

Teaching Notes:

Broken Squares

*Contributed by: Jake Jagel,
Thompson Island Outward
Bound Education Center*

What's Learned
• Cooperation
• Communication
• Problem solving

Equipment
Material needed for each
sub-group of five members.
• One (8-1/2" by 11") manila envelope and five (4"
by 7") envelopes.
• Five (8-1/2" by 11") sheets
of cardboard cut as shown
in diagram A.

Pre-activity Preparation
Cut, mix-up and insert cardboard pieces and instruc-
tions into the 4" by 7"
envelopes (As shown in diagram C) and place them into
the 8-1/2" by 11" envelopes.

Overview
This activity is best presented by having a discussion
on the meaning of "cooperation" prior to the activity.
Listing the behaviors
required to be a cooperative
person is beneficial and can

later be used in the debrief.
This activity is a good pre-
and post-evaluation of the
change in a group's cooperative effort after a series of
initiatives.

Activity Introduction
Inside each envelope are
pieces of a puzzle. The task
is to form five perfect squares
from the envelopes' contents.

Description
The group is divided into
sub-groups of five members.
Distribute one large enve-
lope to each sub-group.
Each person then gets a

smaller envelope containing
three puzzle pieces. At the
signal, the task of the group
is to form five squares of
equal size from the pieces.
The task is not complete
until everyone has a perfect
square and all the squares
are of the same size.

Rules
• No member of the group
may speak.
• No member of the group
may ask for a piece or in
any way signal that one is
wanted.
• Members may exchange
pieces within the group.

Solution
(See Diagram B)

Debriefing Questions
• What skills were needed
to come up with the solu-
tion?
• How did you feel when
someone held a piece and
didn't see the solution?
• What was your reaction
when people finished their
squares and then sat back
without seeing whether
their solutions prevented
others from solving the
problem?
• What were your feelings if
you finished your square
and then realized that you
would have to break it
and give away a piece?
• How did you feel about
the person that was slow
at seeing the solution?
• When you weren't able to
talk, what were the other
ways you were able to
communicate with other
member of the group?

Classroom Application
• Mathematics
• Creative thinking

Teaching Notes:

Diagram A

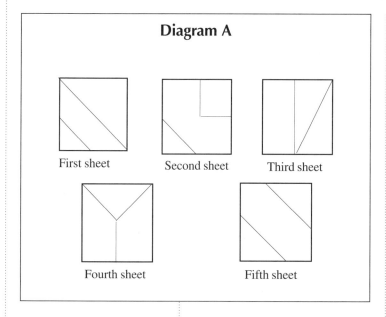

First sheet

Second sheet

Third sheet

Fourth sheet

Fifth sheet

Diagram B

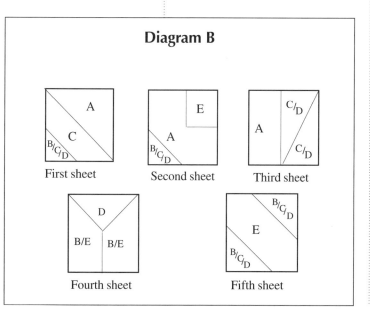

First sheet

Second sheet

Third sheet

Fourth sheet

Fifth sheet

Diagram C

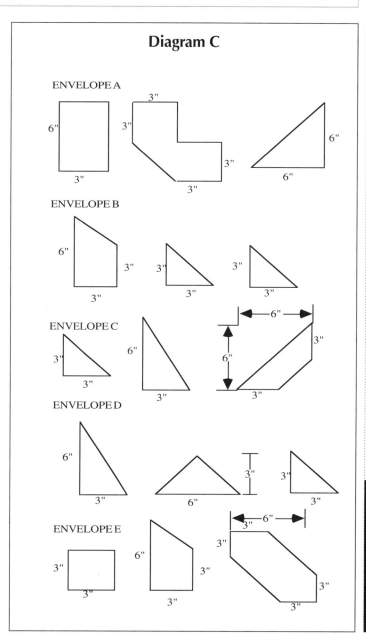

ENVELOPE A

ENVELOPE B

ENVELOPE C

ENVELOPE D

ENVELOPE E

Teaching Notes:

The Monster Race

Contributed by: Phil Costello, Founder and Director of Project U.S.E.

Creator – New Games Foundation, San Francisco, Calif.

What's Learned
- Cooperation
- Trust
- Decision making

Equipment
- None required

Pre-activity Preparation
This activity requires a large, open space free of obstructions or obstacles.

Overview
The Monster Race is intended to be a fun activity best used at the end of a series of initiatives.

Activity Introduction
To keep dragons away from the village, residents would participate in an annual monster race in the dark. The villagers would divide

themselves up, imitate large scary monsters and race against each other. The dragons in the surrounding mountains would hear the race, think real monsters lived in the village and stay away.

Description
Divide the entire group into small groups of equal size. Each group is instructed to create a monster. The monster must make a sound and move from point A to point B, (not more than 20 yards) with only a specified num-

ber of feet and hands allowed to touch the ground. The number of feet is determined 1/3 the total number of feet in the small group (a group size of 10 members is allowed to have 10 feet touching the ground). The correct number of hands is equal to 1/3 of the total hands of the small group (a group of 10 members is allowed to have seven hands touching the ground). The groups start the race with all team members unattached and standing on the ground. The

group members must remain attached at all times. If they come apart, they must reattach before moving forward.

Debrief
- What difficulties did your group experience in creating the monster?
- How did you resolve these difficulties?
- What improvements would you make if you did this activity again?

Classroom Application
- Classmates having fun and interacting.

CHAPTER 6

Developing Awareness Initiatives

These are activities generally presented in a group context but directed toward the individual. The focus is on acknowledgment of values, diversity, aspirations, expectations, compassion, courtesy, and ethics. They require considerable in-depth debriefing so the participants can gain insights and incorporate the experiences into their daily lives. We suggest they be used, not as icebreakers but after members of the group have achieved some level of comfort and trust with each other.

Developing Awareness Initiatives

Quick Reference Chart

Activity Name	What's Learned	Indoor or Outdoor	Minimum No. of Participants	Special Equipment Required	Pre-activity Preparation Required	Classroom Application
Trust Exercises	Trust Support Risk-taking Teamwork	Either	12	Yes	Yes	Classroom sensitivity
Blindfold Initiatives	Communication Trust Support	Either	6	Yes	Yes	Classroom sensitivity Critical thinking
Amoeba Scavenger Hunt	Perseverance Communication Trust Risk-taking	Either	6	Yes	Yes	Building classroom relations
Lapsit	Support Trust Teamwork	Either	5	No	No	Fun
The Creative Process	Communications Risk-taking Expressiveness	Either	3	Yes	Yes	Cooperative learning and peer teaching
Shield	Self-concept Values	Either	3	Yes	Yes	Values Classroom relations Cultural Understanding

Activity Name	What's Learned	Indoor or Outdoor	Minimum No. of Participants	Special Equipment Required	Pre-Activity Preparation Required	Classroom Application
Bomb Shelter	Compassion Self-concept Expressiveness Values	Either	3	No	Yes	Class cohesiveness Values Cultural understanding
Passion and Partnership	Compassion Expressiveness Trust Self-confidence	Either	5	Yes	No	Cooperative learning and peer teaching
Essences	Self-confidence Trust Communication Expressiveness	Either	3	No	No	Cooperative learning and peer teaching
Communication Excercise	Verbal & nonverbal communication Listening	Either	3	No	No	Creativity Communication
The Wheel	Trust Communication skills Risk taking Expressiveness	Either	3	Yes	Yes	Supportive classroom environment

Developing Awareness Initiatives

Quick Reference Chart

Initiatives

Teaching Notes:

Trust Exercises

1.Wind in the Willows
2. Trust Fall

Contributed by: Mitch Sakofs, Outward Bound Inc.

What's Learned
• Trust
• Support
• Risk-taking
• Teamwork

Equipment
• *Wind in the Willows*—None required
• *Trust Fall*—A platform or any flat surface approximately five feet off the ground that can support the weight of the largest person in the group.

Pre-activity Preparation
We recommend instruction in spotting followed by spotting exercises prior to participating in all trust initiatives.

One-on-one spotting is a good lead-up experience. Have participants pair up and stand, front to back. The person in front leans back with the person behind putting her hands up to stop the backward motion. Initially the person catching should have their hands touching the back of the person falling. As trust and skill deepen, the person catching can gradually allow the person to fall further as long as it stays within the falling person's comfort zone. Good communication between partners is essential.

Overview
Having the capacity to trust others and the personal confidence to support others are essential in developing supportive personal relationships. The principal teachings in trust exercises are putting trust in others to provide for your personal safety and trusting yourself to protect others from harm. Trust exercises are uncomplicated yet powerful activities that can be the most anxiety-provoking of all initiatives.

1. Wind in the Willows

Creator – New Games Foundation, San Francisco, Calif.

Pre-activity Preparation
• None required

Activity Introduction
Introduce this activity by describing a picture of a big willow tree standing in an open field swaying gently in a warm summer breeze. Focus on relaxation, freedom and a willingness to let go.

Description
One person stands in the center of a tight circle formed by the other members of the group. Those comprising the circle stand with hands up, outstretched and nearly touching the person in the center. One leg dropped back behind the other creates stability. The person in the middle of the circle stands with a tight body (stiff) and arms crossed in front of his chest. When ready, the person in the center says "Ready to fall," <u>but should not move until the group is ready and responds "Fall."</u> When the group says

76

Teaching Notes:

"Fall" the person in the middle leans to one side and is caught by the group. Then, with care, the group rotates the person around the circle rocking them gently for a minute or so. To finish, the person in the center can simply assert control over his body and thus signal that he would like the exercise to end. At this point, the group makes sure the individual being rotated is stable before relaxing its vigil.

Safety and Special Considerations

This activity requires strict attention to safety. The person in the middle chooses his level of risk by asking the group to move forward or backward to adjust how far they fall. Doing the activity in silence or having the group hum are enjoyable variations.

Debriefing Questions

- How was it?
- Did you feel safety inside the circle? Why or why not?
- What was the risk for in this activity?
- When being asked for support, on what conditions did you give it?

What was it like to ask for support?
- Do you allow or ask for support in your classroom?
- When was the last time you asked for support?
- What did you learn about trust? Is trust needed in the classroom. When?

Academic Application

- Classroom sensitivity

2. Trust Fall

Contributed by: Mitch Sakofs, Outward Bound Inc.

Pre-activity Preparation

This activity requires high levels of trust and is not recommended as an introductory activity. There should be no fewer then 10 participants to conduct this activity safely. The group should practice the positioning of the participants and the falling commands prior to doing the activity.

Description

Have the group form two lines facing each other. Each participant extends her arms out forming an interlocking line of arms that are nearly touching (do not grasp hands). One member of the group stands at the head of the two lines to ensure group positioning is in line with the person to fall. When all catchers are in place and ready to catch, the "faller" stands on the platform, crosses arms over chest (tight body) and falls backward. The following commands should be used to ensure safety.

The individual who is about to fall begins with "READY TO FALL," but does not move until the group responds "FALL" and the name of the individual ("FALL, MARY "). To which the faller responds "FALLING," and then falls backwards. Each Faller is briefed not to sit, and to keep their entire body straight, especially the knees.

Safety and Special Considerations

This activity can be extremely dangerous if the command system is not followed exactly as prescribed. Practice the commands and discuss the sensation of what it feels like when a faller lands in the group's arms. If an individual group member has difficulty with a five-foot high platform, use a lower platform.

Debriefing Questions

- Was it difficult to let go and fall? Why?
- How do you establish trust with others? How did you establish trust in this activity?
- How did it feel to catch the person?
- What are some ways people support each other?
- What does it mean to take a risk? What was the risk for you in this activity?
- How can we support each other in the classroom?

Classroom Application

- Classroom relations building
- Classmate sensitivity

Initiatives

Teaching Notes:

Blindfold Initiatives

1. Blind Line Up
2. Blind Square
3. Blindfold Trust Walks

What's Learned
- Trust
- Support
- Communication

Equipment
One blindfold per group member. "Blind Square" requires a 30' rope.

Pre-activity Preparation
You need an area free of obstructions for these types of activities. Special instruction in caring for another's safety and what that involves should precede all blindfold activities. All blindfold activities require careful supervision by the teacher. Spotting by the teacher may be necessary.

Overview
Blindfold activities develop trust. They provide some understanding of personal comfort levels in relation to leading and following;

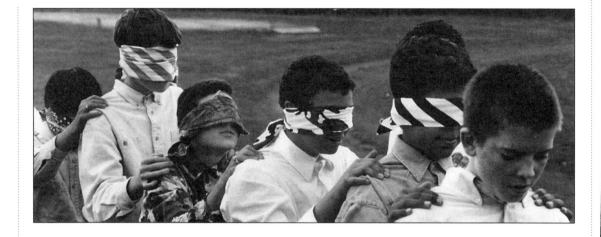

being in control or letting go, and being trusted. They develop increased awareness of various forms of communication.

1. Blind Line-up

Contributed by: John Dutton, Colorado Outward Bound School

Creator – Project Adventure, Hamilton, Mass.

Description
Start by blindfolding the entire group. The group task is to organize and align itself into a straight line according to height, age, or alphabetically by first or last name.

Special Consideration
The teacher needs to be aware of inappropriate touching and discuss touching before the activity starts.

Debriefing Questions
- What difficulties did you experience in aligning yourself with others?
- How did you overcome the difficulties?

2. Blind Square

Contributed by: Debra C. Banks, Colorado Outward Bound School

Creator – Project Adventure, Hamilton, Mass.

Description
The group is blindfolded. The instructor places a rope in everyone's hands, either in front of or behind their backs. The participants may not let go of the rope, although they may let it slide through their hands. They can move in position, but they cannot switch their order or "pass" anyone. The task is to create a perfect square.

Debriefing Questions
- Does being blind mean being powerless?
- Does being blind only mean giving up sight?
- What did you learn about communications?

Teaching Notes:

ClassroomApplication
- Classroom relations building
- Classmate sensitivity

3. Blindfold Trust Walks

Variations:
a) **Group Trust Walk #1**
b) **Group Trust Walk #2**
c) **Trust Walk in Pairs**
d) **The Human Camera**

Contributed by: Mitch Sakofs, Outward Bound Inc.

a) Group Trust Walk #1
Each member of the group is blindfolded and linked together by holding hands. The instructor leads the group over a variety of terrains, walking at a pace that allows the group to travel along safely and together. When the group is feeling comfortable aligned in that order, ask the group to trade places in line and continue the walk.

b.) Group Trust Walk #2
Circle up and explain to the group that they will soon be blindfolded and that, together, they will have to travel from where they are to a spot which you select. Give them five minutes to plan a strategy, blindfold everyone and set them off. Assure them from the outset that you will attend to their safety and not let them bump into anything.

c.) Trust Walk in Pairs
Circle up and explain to the group that each member will be given an opportunity to be blindfolded and led on a walk. Depending on the needs of the group, you may want the experience to be conducted in silence or not. (When conversation is permitted, people tend to get to know each other; when conversation is not permitted, it tends to be a very powerful experience for the individuals who are blindfolded, as they tune into their other senses.) Whether you choose to have it done in silence or not, give directions on this point in the beginning of the exercise to ensure everyone has the same experience.

Have the members of the group form pairs. At this point, discuss some safety issues with the group, such as the need to be aware of the terrain; obstacles that their partners might bump into at knee, shoulder or head level; the walking speed. Alerting people to these issues is important. It is also important to suggest possible activities, for example, sighted person to give objects to her partner to touch or smell.

d.) The Human Camera
Have the group pick partners and develop a nonverbal signal (such as squeezing the hand) at which the sighted person will allow the blindfolded partner an opportunity to see something from a camera-eye view. For example, the sighted person may move her partner into a position where she gets a close-up view of a flower. Once positioned, the sighted people will squeeze their partner's hand for a fraction of a second, and during that time the sightless people are given a glimpse of the flower. At times the sighted people may allow their partners to enjoy a lengthy "time exposure," by squeezing the hand for an extended period of time, or they may also choose to limit the exposure to a fraction of a second by squeezing the hand quickly.

Debriefing Questions
- What was your comfort level at the beginning, middle and end of each activity?
- What skills did people use to communicate with each other?
- What parts of the activity helped you develop trust?
- How can you relate this experience to other parts of your life?

Initiatives

Into The Classroom:

Teaching Notes:

Amoeba Scavenger Hunt

Contributed by : Steven J. Rippe, Voyageur Outward Bound School

What's Learned
- Perseverance
- Communications
- Risk-taking
- Trust

Equipment
- 40 feet of rope
- A set of scavenger hunt directions

Pre-activity Preparation
Prepare the scavenger hunt

site by placing the items to be found in specific locations. It is helpful to have scavenger hunt directions written out and handed to the group. Examples:

- Find someone with a birthday within the past month and sing "Happy Birthday" to her as a group.
- Pass through a tight squeeze to find an object.
- Interview someone and ask him his definition of empowerment.

Overview
Prepare the group by informing them of the physical closeness of this activity and ask for their participa-

tion. Provide alternatives for individuals that choose not to participate. This is an advanced initiative that requires prior activity in a support sequence e.g., Trust Exercises or Blindfold Initiatives. Groups larger than 10 members work better if separated into two groups.

Activity Introduction
The group is lost in a vast kingdom with only a set of directions to locate keys to a puzzle which will point the way home.

Description
Students work together in this activity to form one large organism called an amoeba. The group stays together using a rope wrapped around the outside of the group and tied off, or they can interlock elbows. The group travels to a variety of sites, and participates in a scavenger hunt. Once the hunt is completed, the amoeba finishes its journey by reaching a designated spot.

Rules
When traveling up stairs, or through difficult terrain, the

group must be ready to deal with the complexity, or the instructor must be prepared to assist. Specifically:

- The group must take small steps, no running.
- The group must stay together.
- At any time, any member can shout stop and the group must stop.
- When indoors, the amoeba can only whisper.
- The amoeba can communicate only face-to-face.

Debriefing Questions
- What happened?
- What did you experience?
- How were decisions made?
- Where you able to compete the scavenger hunt? What were your challenges?
- How did the group process make you feel?
- How did you as a team do in the area of: teamwork, risk-taking, problem-solving and tenacity?
- How can you apply what you learned?

Classroom Application
- Classroom relations building.

Teaching Notes:

Lapsit

Contributed by:
Staff, Hurricane Island
Outward Bound School

Creator – New Games
Foundation, San Francisco,
Calif.

What's Learned
• Teamwork
• Support
• Trust

Equipment
None required

Pre-activity Preparation
None required

Overview
A simple, fun activity that clearly illustrates that the whole is greater than its parts.

Activity Introduction
Many years ago in the cold region of Lapvia, Lapvian soldiers would die from resting on the cold, icy, snowy ground. They developed a technique that allowed everyone to rest and to stay warm.

Description
Have the group form a circle, and move close together, so that the participates are touching shoulders. Then do a "Right Face" and move in close, so that people are looking and feeling sandwiched between others in the group. Talk the group into slowly sitting down onto the lap of the person behind them. For support, people can place their hands on the shoulders of the people in front of them.

Variations
• Once people are sitting, have them massage the shoulders of the people in front of them.
• Have the group walk in a circle.
• Have the group lean back.

Debriefing Questions
• Did you trust the people around you? What happened when you didn't?
• What made this activity successful?
• Did you think it was possible at first?
• If the group broke down, what happened?

Classroom Application
• Having fun with classmates.

Initiatives

Teaching Notes:

The Creative Process

Contributed by: Peter H. Bailey, Voyageur Outward Bound School

Creator – Lois Brandt, Art Teacher, New York City

What's Learned
- Communication
- Risk-taking
- Expressiveness

Equipment
- Paper (drawing type; bigger than 8 1/2 by 11 inch) one sheet per participant
- Crayons (five to seven) for the entire group
- A flip chart

Pre-activity Preparation
A quiet, comfortable place with a relaxing atmosphere.

Overview
This activity serves well as an introduction to experiential education for both high school students (juniors and seniors) and adult learners. The activity invites partici-pants to try things in new ways. Processing time is critical.

Activity Introduction
The activity introduction is incorporated into the description.

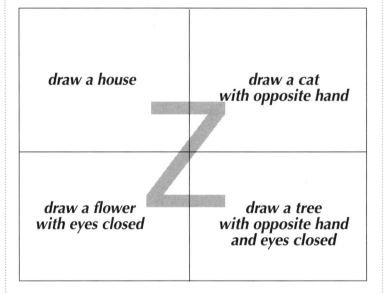

draw a house

draw a cat with opposite hand

draw a flower with eyes closed

draw a tree with opposite hand and eyes closed

Description
Take the paper and fold it in half; then in half again, so that you have four equal boxes. You have 15 sec-onds for each object. To start:
1. Upper left box – draw a house.
2. Upper right box – draw a cat with your opposite hand.
3 Lower left box – draw a flower with eyes closed and the hand you normal-ly write with.
4. Lower right box – draw a tree with your opposite hand and your eyes closed.

After each participant has completed his/her drawing, ask the following questions:
1. Would any of you like to share your drawings, observations, feelings or thoughts about this?
2. Which drawing of the four did you like the most and why?
3. What was different for you in each drawing?
4. Which drawing did you feel the most comfortable with?

Remember, there are no right or wrong answers, but whichever object (house, cat, flower or tree) you liked drawing the best says some-thing about where you are comfortable on the Creative Continuum. (At which point, the instructor draws a big Z connecting all boxes. Then the instructor asks the questions, "Would you all agree that we have the most control of our ability when we drew the house, and the least when we drew the tree?"

Debriefing Questions
- The debriefing is incorpo-rated in the activity.

Classroom Application
- Cooperative learning, Peer teaching and developing creativity

Teaching Notes:

Shield

Contributed by:
John Dutton, Colorado
Outward Bound School

Creator – Sid Simon and
Howard Kirsenbaum,
Values Clarification

What's Learned
• Self-concept
• Values Clarification

Equipment
• paper, pencils
• crayons, markers
• paste and pictures

Overview
This activity helps students evaluate themselves and clarify their personal values.

Activity Introduction
In day-to-day life, choices are arrived at and decisions are made based on what is valued. In many instances, values are hidden and unclear and never surface for clarification.

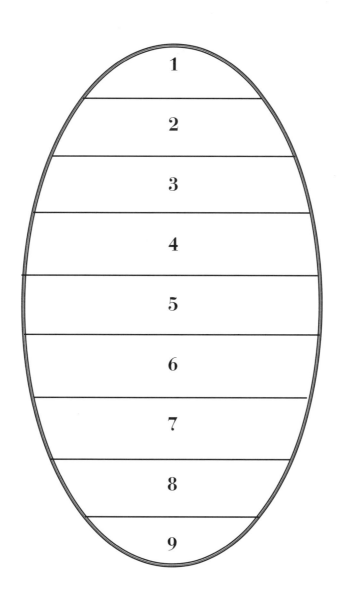

Description
Have each student draw and fill in the following shield. The students can draw or paste magazine pictures on the shield

Debriefing
After each shield is completed, each member presents their shield in front of the group.

Classroom Application
• Classroom relations
• Values
• Cultural understanding

Shield Key

1. *What do I do best?*
2. *What am I trying to get better at?*
3. *My favorite possession.*
4. *My life symbol.*
5. *Greatest success of last 12 months.*
6. *Greatest failure.*
7. *3 words that describe me.*
8. *3 words that I would like people to use to describe me.*
9. *Unrestrained by money and commitments, what wuold I do in the next 12 months?*

Initiatives

Teaching Notes:

Bomb Shelter

*Contributed by
John Dutton
Colorado Outward Bound
School*

*Created by Sid Simon and
Howard Kirsenbaum, Values
Clarification*

What's Learned
• Compassion
• Self concept
• Expressiveness
• Values Clarification

Equipment
A very quiet and comfortable area

Pre-Activity Preparation
None required

Overview
In this activity each person is asked to take on an imaginary role and justify why one should be spared from a nuclear war. You play the part based only upon your personal experiences and values. The bomb shelter activity helps identify those values that are most important to the individual.

Activity Introduction
Create a prepared scenario. Example: The world is about to experience a nuclear war. In your community is a bomb shelter that will hold only six people. In your group of eleven there is a school teacher, a pregnant teenager, a scientist, a teenager with AIDS, a minister, an honor student, a school dropout, a politician, a military leader, and a doctor accompanied by his wife. The scenario can vary depending upon group size and personality and the background of the participants.

Description
The task is to decide among the members of the group which six will enter the bomb shelter.

Special Consideration
This activity needs to be carefully monitored by the instructor. Emotions can run high and individual values are often challenged.

Debriefing Question
• What prejudices surfaced?
• After the activity was explained to you and you were informed of the character you were to play, did you make any assumptions about who would stay and who would leave? For instance:

• What new individual values surfaced as a result of participating?
• Were your early stereotypes accurate?
• From what you learned, what new impressions do you have of your classmates?

Classroom Application
• Values clarification
• Building classroom relations
• Cultural Thinking

Teaching Notes:

Passion and Partnership

Contributed by: Kim Marshall and Peter Bailey, Voyageur Outward Bound School

What's Learned
- Compassion
- Perseverance
- Trust
- Self-confidence
- Self-concept
- Expressiveness

Equipment
- One pad of paper per participant and a pen or pencil
- A very quiet place— a beautiful outdoor setting is best.

Pre-activity Preparation
- None required

Overview
Passion and Partnership is an extended exercise in personal reflection, values clarification, action planning and partnership building. The complete activity requires a minimum of two hours. If the required time is not available, the activity can be segregated into separate time blocks. This activity works best when the participants know each other, and is best suited for high school students or older. A group discussion exploring good partnership relationships at the beginning of the exercise can increase effectiveness. Passion and Partnership should not be used as an introductory exercise or ice-breaker.

Activity Introduction
Start the exercise by creating a reflective mental picture.

Description
Step 1
The teacher says: Relax, be still and let your whole life pass before you. Mentally step back far enough so you can see your whole life's picture to date – from your earliest years to the present moment. Using this mental picture as a resource, answer the following questions on paper, taking care to answer for yourself and not for someone else's expectations of you.

Step 2
In the larger group, each participant shares their list (highlights/insights). The group is responsible for aligning individual members into partners based on similar interests. The newly created partnerships share their circled items in greater detail with each other and identify the following;
- What is holding you back from doing the things you love most?
- What is a reasonable goal for increasing this focus in your life?

Step 3
The individual makes an action plan for addressing the question. The plan should be specific in creating an attainable goal. The individual will need to identify areas in which one can reduce time, energy, and the emotional investment in order to free up time for new priorities.

Step 4
The new partnerships, together, address the question: How can we best support each other in staying focused and adjusting these plans when we return to our regular classroom environments?

Debriefing Questions
The debriefing is incorporated throughout the activity.

Classroom Application
- Cooperative Learning
- Peer Teaching

Initiatives

Teaching Notes:

Essences

Contributed by:
Susan Lincoln,
Hurricane Island Outward
Bound School

Creator – Debra Gore,
Albuquerque, Minn.

What's Learned
• Expressiveness
• Self-concept
• Communication
• Trust

Equipment
• None required.

Pre-activity Preparation
Essences is a exercise in creating positive feedback. It works best with a group in which the individuals know and enjoy each other. It is best introduced at a time when the group is feeling good about itself and the stress level is low. A group size of 10 to 12 is best.

Overview
This game provides a creative and fun way for people to find out what other people think of them and "how they come across." Every-

one is curious as to how he is perceived—this activity provides a structure to hear those perceptions in a non-threatening matter. It creates a setting—a means of telling someone how you see him and offers a method of giving positive strokes to others.

Essences can deepen the trust level among members of a group.

Activity Introduction
None required — incorporated in the description.

Description
Everyone sits in a circle and one person is picked to leave the circle for a few minutes. This person is the Asker. From the remaining members of the group, an It is selected. The Asker is called back into the circle. The Asker's task is to guess

who the It is by asking 3 to 5 questions of the group. The questions are in the form of:
• If this person were an animal, what would he be, and why?
• If this person were a kind of weather, what would she be, and why?

After asking the questions (being as creative as possible, and being descriptive) the Asker guesses the identity of the It person whose essence is being described. Members of the group rotate in and out of various roles. (Exampe: the It becomes an Asker, and so on.

Rules
Care needs to be taken to create a tone that is positive, sensitive and enjoyable.

Debriefing Questions
• The debrief is incorporated in the activity.

Classroom Application
• Cooperative Learning

Teaching Notes:

Communication Exercise

Contributed by: Nanci Ohnesorge, Beech Hill Hospital Adolescent Center, Dublin, New Hampshire

What's Learned
• Empathy
• Listening skills
• Verbal and non-verbal communication

Equipment
• None required

Pre-activity Preparation
None

Overview
This is a great activity to do with a group that is having difficulty listening to each other. It can introduce the concepts of effective communication in a non-threatening and fun manner.

Activity Introduction
Have the participants pair up with the person that they know the least in the group. Have the group form a standing circle with the pairs standing next to each other.

Description
have the standing pairs face each other. The role of the person on the right side of the pair is to tell their partner about their "Dream Vacation." If time and money were not an issue, where would they go? What would they do? Encourage them to be descriptive, but to keep the story clean.

The role of the person on the left side of the pair is to do everything in their power to show their partner that they are *not* listening—except walk away.

Allow them several minutes to experience the full effects of the activity, i.e., until creativity dwindles, frustrations build, etc.

Have the partners change roles and repeat the above instructions.

Stop the group and have repeat the activity with one exception: the person in the non-listening role is now going to do everything in his or her power to show their partner that they are very interested in what they are saying and that they are listening.

Switch roles.

Variations
Have the partners describe their "Dream Automobile."

Rules
• No one can walk away.

Debrief
• Describe their body language.
• How did it feel when your partner was not listening?
• How did you respond to your partner's lack of listening? Walk away? Raise your voice? Lose interest in the story?
• How did you know that your partner was not listening? What did they do that made you believe that they were not listening?
• Describe their body language.
• How did you feel when they listened to each other?
• How did communication change when you listened to each other?

Classroom Application
• Creativity
• Building Classroom Communication

Initiatives

Teaching Notes:

The Wheel

Contributed by: Helen Fouhey, Thompson Island Outward Bound education Center

What's Learned
• Trust
• Communication Skills
• Risk Taking
• Self-expression
• Writing skills

Equipment
• Wheel
• Pen or pencil
• Quiet location for writing

Pre-activity Preparation

The Wheel is most often used as a reflective tool, to debrief an activity or to bring closure to a series of events. The Wheel has become an invaluable tool used to debrief community service projects. The activity is best done right after the service project before students have dispersed. As with any writing activity, it is best for the teacher/facilitator to sit down and write out the wheel along with the students. While it is often difficult to have students write in their journals, the wheel provides a structured personal writing experience and there is enough variety in the questions that even the most reluctant student can participate. Once the students have filled in the wheel, each one is asked to share something from their wheel. It is what individuals choose to read that determines their level of risk. Instructions for writing should be specific, encouraging students to name particular situations or individuals in their wheel.

Activity Introduction

This activity provides enough structure to allow students to reflect on their activities in a non-threatening way. Asking students to read their writing out loud requires others to listen and give respect; hearing friends give thoughtful and heartfelt accounts of an activity inspires others to "upgrade" their answers to the level of real feelings. Reflection is of critical importance to learning and this type of activity can be adapted widely to any type of activity both in

Developing Awareness Initiative

Teaching Notes:

an out of the classroom; categories can be renamed, shapes redrawn, etc. The Wheel is now included as a portfolio piece on community service at one local high school.

Description

"I am passing out a piece of paper, it is called The Wheel. As you can see, there are a number of slices in the wheel. Each slice has a label (read examples of labels). Examples of labels include:
• Something I learned about myself;
• Something I learned about someone else;
• Something that surprised me about the activity we did;
• A high point;
• A low point, etc.

What I would like you to do is to fill out the wheel using the community service activity that we did today. For example: The high point of my day was when Antonio read *The Little Engine That Could* to the first grade boys. I felt so proud of him and so impressed by his gentleness with the children." Give

several examples so that the students really get the picture. Give students 10 to 15 minutes to write, checking in as soon as people begin to get restless. If over half of the group is done and you

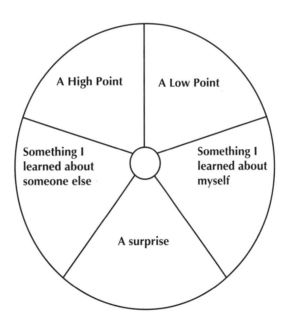

are beginning to lose the group, begin sharing around the circle telling those not finished they can add things as the group goes on. Each person can share one category of their choice. The sharing can continue until the facilator feels the debrief

has accomplished its goals. The center of the wheel is a circle and students can draw a symbol that best represents how they feel during the activity. Begin with someone who will set a positive

and somewhat serious tone for the group. It is not that laughter can not be part of this activity, but it is important that everyone feels safe enough to share sensitive feelings and thoughts. You can start if you can not figure out who else should.

Debrief

The Wheel can be used for a variety of activities and saved in a student's portfolio. At the end of the year, students can share from several wheels as a way to look back over a year. As a group gains more trust and respect for each other, wheels will become more personal. That is an especially powerful progression for students and teachers to witness. Debriefing is part of the activity.

Classroom Application
• Developing classroom relationships.
• Writing skills

Initiatives

Teaching Notes:

Cave In Simulation

Contributed by: Jon Mark Howard, Hurricane Island Outward Bound School

Creator – Sid Simon and Howard Kirsenbaum, Values Clarification

What's Learned
Compassion
Self concept
Values Clarification
Support

Equipment
A space where it can appear dark. If the activity is conducted in a classroom, place tables and chairs in the room to create a maze of sorts that the group will have to navigate. If the activity is conducted outside, be sure there are objects that the group will have to navigate around, over or under. Sometimes rope can assist in this process, although it is not required.

There should be a space large enough for the entire group to be able to sit down in a circle.

Pre-Activity Preparation
The teacher should arrange the room with tables and chairs to create the maze. Whether done outside or inside, the teacher should have the route planned out for traveling into the cave.

Candles should be readily available for the activity. Tone setting is a key factor. Having the space dark helps to create the feeling of being in a cave. Gesture and movement to indicate walking in a cave also helps to create a tone that makes the activity more successful.

Overview
In this activity the participant is asked to look at his self worth in the context of where he is now and the particular group he is with.

Activity Introduction
Explain to the group that they are about to go on a caving expedition and that they will need to line up in single file behind you so that it will be safe to go caving.

Description
With one candle lit, the teacher begins to take the group on a trip through "the cave." The teacher leads students around and under objects, takes big steps to simulate gaps in "the rock," and turns sideways to simulate "a ledge. This walk should take approximately five or ten minutes. At the end of the walk, the teacher will have led the group into a place that is designated as "the cave" and asks all of the students to sit down in a circle facing each other. At this point, the teacher might light the other candles.

The teacher would then explain that there has been an accident and on their way into the cave they knocked over some rocks that are going to make it difficult for all members of the group to get back out. The teacher then states that each person in the group needs to decide where they think they should be in the line going back and why. The teacher further informs the students that this decision is based on the fact that the further back a person is in the line, the less likely he is to make it back out of the cave. The teacher informs the students that because he was responsible for getting

the students into this situation in the first place, the teacher will be the last person in line.

After each person has had time to think, a candle will be passed around. Each person will state to the group where they would like to be in the line and why. After this has occurred, the group must decide on the placement of each person. The group then will get into the line agreed upon and begin their journey back out of the cave.

A discussion of the experience occurs after the activity is over.

Solution
All students make it back out of the cave.

Special Considerations
This can be a very emotional activity depending on the trust level within the group. The teacher needs to be aware of where each student is during this activity and be prepared to follow up with individuals if necessary. Students should be given the option to pass if they do not wish to share any information. There are many varia-

Teaching Notes:

tions to set a lighter tone for this activity. Teachers should assess the group and review variations noted below.

Variations

Have the students decide one or two things they have to live for. Upon deciding on these items, they share them with the rest of the group. The teacher makes it clear that all students will make it back out of the cave. Other students or the teacher can provide information if needed.

Have the students think about what "tools/skills" they have. Upon arrival at the cave, explain that this dark, cold, wet cave represents one of the following: their school, their classroom, or some other problem they may have. The cave, in essence, is a symbol for something else. Explain that, in order to get out of the cave, they need to:

- Identify tools/skills they bring to the group to work as a team.
- Apply the metaphor of being in the cave to identified problems in school or home. Brain-storm and

then begin to focus on one.
- Consider and decide what tools/skills could be used to solve the identified problem?
- Come up with solutions to leave the identified problem in the cave.

Discuss all of this with the group. Summarize and then leave the cave when a plan to resolve the problem has been achieved. The plan should include how it will actually be executed. The teacher and students should be prepared to come back and revisit the plan at a later date to assess how it worked.

Another adaptation would be to identify their tools/skills and how those could be used to get the entire group out of the cave. The teacher and other students can assist a student who may be stuck in identifying his or her tools/skills.

Debrief Questions
- What did you learn about your tools/skills?
- What did you learn about utilizing available resources?
- What was it like to move

from the cave back to the outside?
- How did you utilize your skills to resolve the problem and to make a plan?
- How do you think the plan will work?
- What did you learn about supporting others?
- What was it like for you when you saw the last person come back out of the cave?
- What did you first think when you heard you might be stuck in the cave?
- What did you think when you heard some people had less of a chance to make it back out than others?
- How did the group support individuals?
- How did the group do with listening to each person and making decisions based on this information?
- Was it hard to make decisions about where people were to be placed in the line?
- How can the group continue to use the tools/skills that they now have?

Classroom Application
- Class cohesiveness
- Critical thinking
- Decision-making skills

Initiatives

91

CHAPTER 7

Problem-Solving Initiatives

These are the most complex of all initiative activities. They generally require considerable pre-activity preparation and may employ constructed components. The problem-solving skills that are practiced include: planning, cooperation, leadership, risk-taking, teamwork, trust, ingenuity and perseverance.

Photo Left: **The Outward Bound ropes course initiative develops a sense of self-confidence and teamwork.**

Initiatives

93

Problem Solving Initiatives

Quick Reference Chart

Activity Name	What's Learned	Indoor or Outdoor	Minimum No. of Participants	Special Equipment Required	Pre-Activity Preparation Required	Classroom Application
Endless Circle	Trust Perseverance Communication	Either	2	Yes	No	Testing ideas
The Store	Leadership Communication Teamwork Support	Outdoors	6	No	Yes	Health Marketing Economics
All Aboard	Teamwork Cooperation Communication	Either	6	Yes	Yes	Creativity
Flash Flood	Leadership Teamwork	Either	5	Yes	Yes	Exploring options
Nine Cartons	Teamwork Posing Options Decision Making Planning	Either	6	Yes	Yes	Cooperative learning and Mathematics
Spider's Web	Trust Support Teamwork	Either	5	Yes	Yes	Planning Skills
Blind Man's Cure	Communications Teamwork	Outdoors	8	Yes	Yes	Exploring options and planning skills

Problem Solving Initiatives

Quick Reference Chart

Activity Name	What's Learned	Indoor or Outdoor	Minimum No. of Participants	Special Equipment Required	Pre-Activity Preparation Required	Classroom Application
Log Jam	Group dynamics Communication	Either	7	Yes	Yes	Communication
Traffic Jam	Communication Cooperation Planning Sequencing	Either	6	Yes	Yes	Cooperative learning Developing resources
Toxic Waste	Cooperation Teamwork Leadership Group dynamics	Either	5	Yes	Yes	Cooperative learning Developing resources
The M&M Game	Cooperation vs. Competition	Indoors	6	Yes	Yes	Classroom cooperation
Cultural Bridge	Race relations Perseverance	Either	6	Yes	Yes	Geography Social Studies History
Acid River	Brainstorming Teamwork	Either	5	Yes	Yes	Brainstorming
Point A to Point B	Teamwork	Either	5	Yes	Yes	Creating and idea Implementation

Initiatives

Teaching Notes:

Endless Circle

Contributed by: Peter H. Bailey, Voyageur Outward Bound School

What's Learned
- Perseverance
- Trust
- Communication

Equipment
- Strong string or parachute cord.

Pre-activity Preparation
Cut the string into four- to five-foot lengths. The instructor may wish to preface the activity with a briefing session on trust and cooperation.

Overview
A good activity to start the process of people working together. Be alert to participants with low frustration tolerance. Spotting may be required as participants work themselves into pretzels.

Activity Introduction
Make the statement, "Something that seems

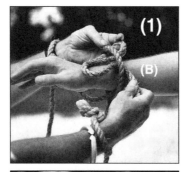
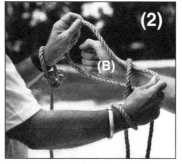

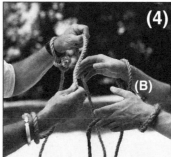

impossible may be very simple if you just stop and think about what you are doing."

Description
Link the string to the wrist of each participant and through the string of the opposite participant. The task is to unlink the participants.

Variation
Try tying the whole group together.

Rules
You cannot cut the string or untie or remove the string looped on the wrist.

Solution
Slip the string through the wrist loop of B, under the backside of the wrist of B and step back. You can give the clue, "A bird in the The hand." When we make quick generalizations, we often miss what is different about the new problem

Debriefing Questions
- What did it feel like tied to the other person?
- As a partnership, how did you resolve the problem?
- Describe your role as a partner, i.e., passive, aggressive, leader, follower, etc.
- How could you relate the activity to participation in a classroom setting?

Classroom Application
- Testing Ideas
- Problem Solving

Teaching Notes:

The Store

Contributed by:
Phil Costello,
Founder and Director of
Project U.S.E.

What's Learned
- Leadership
- Communication
- Teamwork
- Decision Making

Equipment
- $7.89 per group of 10 participants

Pre-activity Preparation
It is recommended that the supermarket manager be advised prior to entering the store.

Overview
A creative way to explore a supermarket, learn about problem-solving, and buy a lunch.

Activity Introduction
Introduce the activity by asking the group question. "How much money do you think it would cost to feed this group?" Record the answer for discussion during the debrief.

Description
In front of a supermarket, a group of 10 individuals is given $7.89. The challenge to the group is to buy lunch for all the participants. The total price of the lunch cannot be below $7.69 and cannot exceed $7.89. The store management should be notified before you enter the store.

Variation
Team members are paried with one blindfolded person and only the blindfolded person selects the food.

Rules
- The meal must be nutritional and must feed the entire group.
- The task must be completed in five minutes with no talking in the supermarket.

Debriefing Questions
- How did the group initially approach this problem?
- What obstacles did you encounter in the store?
- How did the group resolve them?
- What did you observe about leadership?

Classroom Application
- Health Education
- Marketing
- Economics
- Arithmetic

Initiatives

Teaching Notes:

All Aboard

Contributed by: John Dutton, Colorado Outward Bound School

Creator – Project Adventure, Hamilton, Mass.

What's Learned
• Creativity
• Teamwork
• Cooperation
• Communication

Equipment
A large flat surface approximately 24-inches square, 18 to 24 inches off the ground. In the outdoors, a large rock or tree stump is suitable. A string or hula hoop can be substituted for the tree stump.

Pre-activity Preparation
Select an area that is free of surrounding obstructions. Instruction and practice in proper spotting technique prior to participation.

Overview
This activity is a simple and light introduction to the development of teamwork and planning.

Activity Introduction
In two minutes, a flash flood will come running down this canyon and the only way to save the group is to get everyone on the platform.

Description
The goal is to get the entire group on top of the flat surface for 30 seconds.

Variations
• Time it.
• Have everyone sing a song while they're "All Aboard."
• Use smaller and smaller surfaces.
• Do it without talking.
• Have the group plan without talking.

Rules
• No one can sit on the shoulders of anyone.
• No part of any bodies may be touching the ground.

Debriefing Questions
• Did you have a plan?
• What was it?
• Did everyone know what the plan was?
• How many solutions did the group throw out before it settled on one?
• Were people careful with each other?
• What did individuals need or offer to balance other group members?

Classroom Application
• Creativity

Teaching Notes:

Flash Flood

Contributed by: Phil Costello, Founder and Director of Project U.S.E.

- What's Learned
- Leadership
- Teamwork
- Communication

Equipment
- Three logs or posts, 4″ in diameter and approximately 8′ long.
- Three to four smaller logs or posts, 2″ in diameter.
- One section of 1/4″ rope approximately 20′ long.
- One section of 1/2″ rope approximately 30′ long.

Pre-activity Preparation
Prepare the activity site by leaving the equipment scattered about out of sight of the group. It is important that the instructor set the scene by telling a story about the impending flash flood. Spotting is required.

Overview
This is an excellent lead-up activity to more advanced team-building exercises. The instructor can start to

make observations of group members and draw them out in follow-up activities. As this is a construction project, a watchful eye to ensure the participant's safety is a must.

Activity Introduction
A flash flood is coming and to save the group, the members need to be off the ground.

Description
With the materials provided and within 10 minutes, they must construct something to get the entire group at least two feet off the ground.

Rules
Each member of the group must be at least two feet off the ground for at least one minute. A group member cannot be lifted and held off the ground by another group member, but members can be supported or held by another member.

Solution
Create a tripod out of the logs by lashing them together with the 1/4 inch rope. Tie the 1/2 inch rope around the tripod approximately 18 to 24 inches off the ground to create a rail. The group stands on the rope rail holding the center of the tripod and each other.

Debriefing Questions
How did you feel about having your ideas accepted or rejected?
What were the different leadership styles?

Classroom Application
- Creative thinking
- Exploring options

Initiatives

Teaching Notes:

Nine Cartons

Contributed by: Jake Jagel, Thompson Island Outward Bound Education Center

What's Learned
- Teamwork
- Posing Options
- Decision Making
- Planning Skills

Equipment
Lumber specifications:
- Four pieces: 1"x 2" x 5'10-1/2"
- Four pieces: 1"x 2" x 8'4-3/4"
- Four pieces: 1"x 2" x 12'
- Nine cardboard cartons approx.: 13" x 13" x 13"

Pre-activity Preparation
Set-up the first square for each group according to diagram A.

Overview
An excellent indoor problem-solving activity. The group needs to have a minimum of six participants.

Activity Introduction
Before the group is an enormous time bomb set to go off in 10 minutes. To defuse the bomb, the group must construct two squares inside the existing square.

Description
The task is to construct, with the lumber provided, two square-shaped enclosures inside the existing one so that all cartons are isolated from each other.

Solution
See diagram B

Debriefing Questions
- What problems did you encounter during the planning process?
- What leadership style was demonstrated?
- What math skills did you use?

Classroom Application
- Mathematics
- Cooperative learning

Diagram A

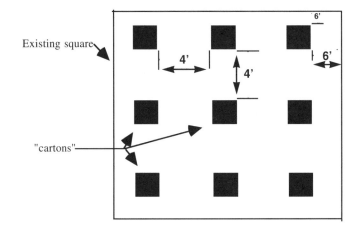

Diagram B

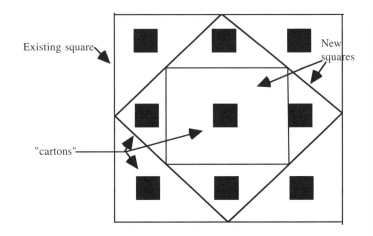

Teaching Notes:

This is an example of one possible web. Volleyball poles can be used in lieu of a tree. Create the Spider Web hole sizes to accommodate the people in the group. It is always good to have a few extra holes.

Spider's Web

Contributed by: John Dutton, Colorado Outward Bound School

Creator – Project Adventure, Hamilton, MA

What's Learned
- Trust
- Support
- Teamwork

Equipment
- One-hundred feet of parachute cord or heavy string

Pre-activity Preparation
Create the Spider Web similar to the photograph.

Overview
This activity requires a considerable amount of planning, cooperation, and teamwork. The Spider Web is a fairly complex initiative and should not be used as an initial activity.

Activity Introduction
The group is standing before a great spider's web. The group must get to the other side by passing through the web without touching it

Description
Everyone starts on one side of the web. Explain that their goal is to move everyone through the web without touching it. Once a hole is used, it is used up and thus cannot be used again. No one may go over the top, around the side or underneath the web. It is forbidden to touch the web. At this point various consequences can be introduced for touching the web, e.g., everyone must go back to the beginning; or perhaps only half must go back. As the leader you may empow-er the group to be its own quality assurance inspectors, choose to take on that role yourself, or assign that role to a member of the group.

Variations
- Time limits.
- Do it without talking.
- Work with two groups with one on the opposite side of the web from the other and going in opposite directions.

Safety
Spotting is required, as people are being lifted off the ground.

Debriefing Questions
- What different roles did individual group members play in the planning process?
- What was the process for posing options?
- What were the difficulties in executing the plans?
- How were those difficulties resolved?
- How did the group work together?

Classroom Application
- Analysis
- Planning skills

Initiatives

Teaching Notes:

Blind Man's Cure

Contributed by: Chris Carrigan, Thompson Island Outward Bound Education Center

What's Learned
- Communication
- Teamwork

Equipment
- Class (four or more depending on how you structure it).
- Blindfolds (enough to blindfold most everyone in the group).
- 75' of 100' climbing rope
- 16' of 1" tubular webbing
- Approximately 37' of rope (to make a circle approximately 12' in diameter)
- Climbing Helmet (at least one)
- A can (No. 01 or something smaller if you would like)
- The "cure" (an item to be placed in the can for the group to retrieve, e.g., candy, an egg—be creative).

Pre-activity Preparation
Step 1: Select activity site

Step 2: Write clues. (Read the sample clues to get a sense of the activity and the kind of clues and consequences you might want to incorporate into your lesson).

Step 3: Place equipment and clues at each site.

Overview
Though better used outdoors, in a pinch this team development and problem-solving initiative can be played indoors. It does require some physical exertion, a complement of equipment and some pre-planning to ensure the activities are appropriate for the group and environment. It works well with groups of 8 to 12 or more people

Activity Introduction
This activity presents a group with a sequence of challenges. After a brief introduction to the activity by the facilitator, the group will be handed a clue directing them to an activity site. At the site they will find a message describing an activity which they must do. Once the activity is completed, the clue will direct the group to the next activity site. The activities presented at each site can be simple or complex and to add challenge a disabling condition can be introduced to one or more members of the team as a consequence for actions taken or rule violations. Though the choice of activities at each site can vary, the primary activity will require creative problem solving, as well as some construction and lifting.

Description
Step 1: Have the group form a circle (We take it for granted, but remember it is a great model to promote effective communication and lots of folks do not use it).

Step 2: Discuss safety factors (the facilitator is the final arbiter of safety, though it should be a responsibility of each member of the group to ensure the safety of all. Remember, too, that safety includes the realm of physical as well as emotional well- being).

Step 3: Hand someone in the group the first clue and send them off. (Again, this clue should have been prepared ahead of time and tailored to the program site.)

Step 4: Shadow the group to ensure safety and "stop action" as needed to keep the group focused, productive, safe and operating in accordance with the rules.

Sample Clues
Clue 1: You are about to embark on a journey of untold adventure. Your mission is to locate and retrieve the capsule that contains the secret to "???????" (Your choice here—educational reform, productivity, whatever.) Your team will be faced with many challenges along the way, so remember—safety first. If your team travels approximately 100 yards due South from where you are now standing, you will find Clue No. 2.

Clue 2: Congratulations!!! You have found the first clue....that is the good news. The bad news is that the first person who touched Clue No. 2 is now blind. At this

Problem-Solving Initiative

Teaching Notes:

capsule from the center of the pool. Remember this: Only the fingers of the blind person may touch the capsule. Use the resources provided.

Solution

Secure the center of the rope to the tree so that the two ends are the same length and can be maneuvered over the toxic circle. Using the webbing, create a lattice between the tow ropes. The blind person lies down in the lattice and is maneuvered over the toxic waste site. Do not forget to have the person in the lattice wear a helmet and to make sure that everyone is caring for each other and the person suspended over the pit.

Debriefing

• How did you treat the blind person?
• How did that person feel?
• How did you make decisions?
• Did you utilize your resources?
• Did you focus on the task? Process? Yourself?

Classroom Application

• Exploring Options

time, please blindfold this individual.

Now form a circle and consider the following questions: 1) What worked well for your team in locating Clue No. 2? What could you have done differently to improve the effectiveness of your team?

What steps will you take to make these improvements? Once you have

completed your discussions, read on.

If you are thinking of North, it is better not to set forth. The South and East ...are not fit for man, woman or beast. Ah...but the West—that is best. Look for Station No. 1 and the fire hose you will find. Now just look a little further...just behind.

Clue 3: Well done. You are now standing on the edge of a pool of toxic slime filled with various types of nasty, gnarly, twisted critters. In the center of the pool floats the capsules that contain the secret "????" (Educational reform—your choice here.) Anyone that touches inside the pool will suffer instant blindfoldness.

Your task is to retrieve the

Teaching Notes:

Islands

Contributed by:
Phil Costello,
Founder and Director of
Project U.S.E.

What's Learned
- Perseverance
- Leadership
- Teamwork
- Trust
- Communications

Equipment
- 3 platforms
- Two 3' x 3' and one 1' x 1' approximately 12" high. (The platforms can vary in size as long as one is slightly smaller than the other two. The height of the platform should never be more than 12" to 18" for safety reasons.)
- (1) 2"x 6" 12'
- (1) 2"x 6" 4'
- The platforms can be constructed from 2" x 4" plywood.

Pre-activity Preparation
A smooth, level surface, either indoors or outdoors is required. Prior to participation, group discussion of developing a planning

process and teamwork is beneficial. During the activity, spotting may be required.

Overview
This is an excellent group problem solving activity. Planning and teamwork are a necessity for successful completion. Participants must take responsibility for their own behavior and also be a productive members of the group. Posing options, testing limits, cooperation, patience and perseverance are skills to be learned through participation. A group size of 10 to 12 is best.

Activity Introduction
The entire group is standing on the first island and must

cross to the other side so that they can get water and continue on their journey.

Description
The group stands on the first of three platforms placed 14 feet apart in a straight line. The first and the last platforms are of equal size; the middle platform is smaller. The group is given a 12–foot board and a 4–foot board to use as aids in crossing from one platform to the next. The task is completed when the entire group is standing on the last platform.

Rules
If any member of the group or either of the boards touches the ground, the entire group starts over from the first platform.

Solution
The entire group stands on the first platform. The short board is extended out resting on the platform with the group standing on it to provide support. The large board is extended from the small one and resting on the smaller, middle platform creating a planking system. A portion of the group moves to the center and the process is repeated until the entire group stands on the end platform.

Debriefing Questions
- What were the obstacles in completing the task?
- How were options processed?
- What did you feel like when an individual caused the group to return to the first platform?
- Ask yourself—were you a leader or just along for the exercise, and did you choose your role?

Classroom Application
- Analytical thinking
- Posing options
- Testing plans

Teaching Notes:

Log Jam

Contributed by: Debra C. Banks , Colorado Outward Bound School –Professional Development Manual

Creator – Project Adventure, Hamilton, Mass.

What's Learned
• Group dynamics
• Communication

Equipment
• A low log or beam about 6" high and 16" wide and 12' long.
• Curbs can work if they are raised on both sides.

Pre-activity Preparation
Select a site; watch out for beams that are too high.

Activity Introduction
Giving no criteria as to how the group should organize itself, ask everyone to stand on a low beam (log, low wall). (If they ask how they should organize, say it doesn't matter yet.)

Description
The task is to reorganize the group according to some

criterion, such as height or age.

Rules
No member of the group is allowed to touch the ground or lift another. Consequences for infractions of the rules include starting the activity from the beginning or putting blindfolds on participants.

Debriefing Questions
• What made this activity difficult?
• What were your keys to success?
• What was the group's problem-solving style? Did it work?
• How were strategies chosen?
• What is it about the nature of an activity that deter-

mines the leadership needs?

Classroom Application
• Planning
• Communications

Initiatives

Into The Classroom:

Teaching Notes:

Traffic Jam

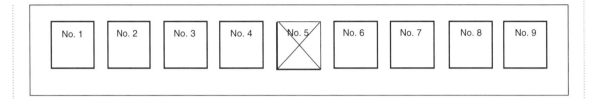

No. 1 | No. 2 | No. 3 | No. 4 | No. 5 | No. 6 | No. 7 | No. 8 | No. 9

Contributed by: John Dutton, Colorado Outward Bound School

Creator – Project Adventure, Hamilton, Mass.

What's Learned
• Group dynamics
• Communication
• Cooperation

Equipment
Poster board, chalk, tape or anything to create a square for standing on.

Pre-activity Preparation
Create a line of squares on the ground; a minimum of six or eight is preferable.

Overview
This is a difficult problem-solving activity which should not be used as an icebreaker. It can take as little as 10 minutes and as long as two hours. Watch and monitor frustration levels.

Activity Introduction
This activity does not require an introduction. It is best just to start with the participants standing on the squares. It usually reduces frustration level to have students start off the squares to allow for planning.

Description
Two groups (four to six people each) facing each other must exchange places on a line of squares, there being one more square than people in the groups. The objective is for the two groups to change sides.

Variations
Do it without talking.
Mute certain people.

Rules
• You may only move forward.
• Only one person may move at a time.
• You can only move two ways: into a free space in front of you or around the person facing you into an empty space.
• You may not leave the grid to solve the problem or use props.
• If you are stuck, you may begin again, having rotated the two front people to the back of the line.
• Sides must move in order:

Solution
1. No. 6 to No. 5
2. No. 4 to No. 6
3. No. 3 to No. 4
4. No. 5 to No. 3
5. No. 7 to No. 5
6. No. 8 to No. 7
7. No. 6 to No. 8
8. No. 4 to No. 6
9. No. 2 to No. 4
10. No. 1 to No. 2
11. No. 3 to No. 1
12. No. 5 to No. 3
13. No. 7 to No. 5
14. No. 9 to No. 7
15. No. 8 to No. 9
16. No. 6 to No. 8
17. No. 4 to No. 6
18. No. 2 to No. 4
19. No. 3 to No. 2
20. No. 5 to No. 3
21. No. 7 to No. 5
22. No. 6 to No. 7
23. No. 4 to No. 6
24. No. 5 to No. 4

Debriefing Questions
• How did you arrive at the solution to the problem?
• Was there a leader?
• How was that person or people chosen?
• Was the group willing to make mistakes, start over, and try again? Or, was it cautious and careful to get it perfect the first time through?
• What are the pros and cons of each approach?
• What was the key to its success?

Classroom Application
• Analysis
• Creative thinking

Teaching Notes:

Toxic Waste

Contributed by: Debra C. Banks, Colorado Outward Bound School, Professional Development Manual

What's Learned
- Cooperation
- Teamwork
- Group Dynamics
- Leadership Styles

Equipment
- A large space in which to lay out a circle with a 25' diameter.
- Two pieces of string/rope 25' long.
- Two #10 cans or something similar.
- An old tire, inner-tube or something similar, e.g., inch-wide sections of a car tire tube.
- One length string 50 feet long.
- Water (food coloring or tomato juice optional to represent the toxic waste).
- 10 pieces of quarter inch rope 25' long.
- Four blindfolds (optional).
- An assortment of unnecessary things

Pre-activity Preparation
Using the 50' string, lay out a large circle. Fill one No.10 can about half way with water, food coloring, tomato juice, etc. Place both No.10 cans in the approximate center of the large circle and separate them by about three to four feet.

Activity Introduction
Bring the group to the circle and explain that they are a toxic waste removal team and their task is to pour the contents of the can filled with toxic waste into the containment unit, i.e., the recovery can. Explain that because budgets are tight, they will have only the following materials to work with (show them the rope, tire tube and other materials) and that the nature of the substances being handled is

so toxic that they must work outside of the danger zone defined by the large circle formed by the string. If at any time anyone reaches into the circle, that person will be blinded.

Description
The task is to pour the toxic waste from one No.10 can to the recovery can. The instructor should keep a watchful eye to ensure rules are being followed, or may elect to establish a regulatory agency to monitor the operation. Individuals who break the vertical plane of the circle are blindfolded.

Variations—Cup of Dreams
Ask each member to write down a dream that they have, professional or personal. Put these into a small cup. Instead of using the Toxic Waste scenario, let the participants know that their objective is to move the cup of dreams from the present to the Window of Opportunity, i.e., the other can. If the cup falls, then a dream is pulled out, and consequently, is thrown out. All other rules apply, but

may need rewording.

Another variation is to have two separate circles that are 50 to 100 feet apart. The can with the toxic waste is placed in the middle of one and the recovery can in the other. The object is to have the group move and pour the toxic waste into the recovery can

Debriefing Questions
- What strengths were in the group to complete the task?
- Did someone have a vision? Was it clearly understand by everyone? Why? Why not?
- What obstacles did the group have to overcome to complete the task?

Debriefing of Variation
- Let each group share what dream they left in the cup.
- Ask members to identify the obstacles to achieving their dreams.

Classroom Application
- Developing resources
- Cooperative Learning
- Science
- Environmental Education

Initiatives

Teaching Notes:

The
M&M Game

Contributed by:
Lewis Glenn,
Outward Bound Inc.

What's Learned
• Cooperation vs. competition
• Teamwork

Equipment
• A very large bag of M&Ms
• One table and two chairs (optional).

Pre-activity Preparation
None required.

Overview
This activity provides a great opportunity to examine and respond to a situation in a non-normal manner that provides positive results. It teaches the value of cooperation and teamwork over competition.

Activity Introduction
Start by asking the group the following: It has been said that competing and competition bring out the best in everyone. Does competition between two groups

ensure that one group will perform at a higher level?

Description
Divide the group into pairs of physically similar or equal partners, i.e., same height and weight, approximately the same strength. Have them lie prone on the ground facing each other, or seat them opposite each other at a table. Separate M&Ms into piles of 10 each. Pairs of participants arm wrestle for M&Ms. Each time one of the pair pushes the other's hand and forearm to the ground (or table), he/she gets to eat one M&M from their pile. If the pair

actually competes against each other, they will work hard to eat their M&Ms. If they think creatively and choose to cooperate by merely taking turns at allowing their partner to push their hand and forearm down, competitors are transformed into collaborators, and they get to eat all the M&Ms.

Rules
The participants are told that the aim of the activity is to acquire and eat as many M&Ms as possible. They can eat M&Ms only when they succeed in pushing the other person's hand and

forearm to the ground (or table) while arm wrestling. They begin the activity when the facilitator says "begin."

Solution
The solution is to cooperate, not to compete. At least one participant in each pair must look at the problem creatively and realize that if the pair cooperates, they can get all the M&Ms that are available. If they continue to compete, they will work hard (arm wrestling) and acquire the M&Ms gradually. If they decide to cooperate, they will alternate getting and eating M&Ms.

If none of the participants reachs the solution, then the facilitator should call a halt after 10 minutes, explain the activity again and let the participants try it again for another 10 minutes.

Debriefing Questions
• When did you realize the real problem?
• What made you stop and start to think about the problem?

Classroom Application
• Classroom cooperation

Teaching Notes:

Acid River

Contributed by: Peter Bailey, Voyageur Outward Bound School

What's Learned
• Shared vision
• Brainstorming
• Teamwork

Equipment
• Three 2″ x 6″ or 2″ x 8″ boards, 8′ long.
• Six cinder blocks (4″ blocks preferred over 8″ blocks).
• A length of rope (10′) can be added, but is not necessary.
• Two pieces of rope 10′ long

Pre-activity Preparation
Select a level area, either indoors or outdoors. Create the acid river using the two 10-foot lengths of string to represent the outline of the river bank. Place the cinder blocks between the river banks according to the diagram.

Overview
A barrier that often precludes effective teamwork is

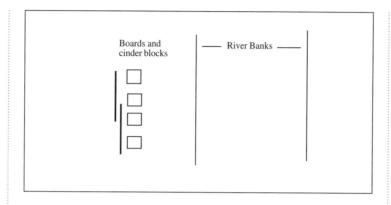

Boards and cinder blocks — River Banks —

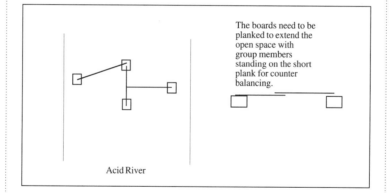

The boards need to be planked to extend the open space with group members standing on the short plank for counter balancing.

Acid River

a lack of clarity about the goal. The goal for this activity is to develop a process, not a product. To be successful, each member of the group must participate to implement an effective plan.

Activity Introduction
The group must cross from one river bank to the opposite bank over the acid river using only the special cinder block islands and the boards.

Description
The task is achieved when the entire group stands on the opposite bank. The group size should not exceed 15 members. Allow 45 minutes to one and a half hours for completion.

Variation
With large groups, have the group members split into two groups, each group starting on opposite banks. If the group is well organized, try using only 4 cinder blocks.

Rules
No part of the participants can touch the acid water. The boards cannot touch the acid water. If a participant on a board touches the acid water, the group must start over. An option to having the entire group start again is if a member touches the water, then that person must be blindfolded.

Debriefing Questions
• How did you feel when fellow group members made mistakes and caused the group to go back to the start?
• Which types of school situations resemble an acid river?

Classroom Application
• Brainstorming
• Cooperative learning

Initiatives

Into The Classroom:

Teaching Notes:

Cultural Bridge

Contributed by: Rick Gordon, Hurricane Island Outward Bound School

What's Learned
- Race relations
- Perseverance
- Communication

Equipment
- Dixie cups
- Two bed sheets
- Newsprint
- Egg cartons
- Paper clips
- Tape

Pre-activity Preparation
Hang the two sheets; the first creates the fog bank and the second provides a barrier so that the other team cannot see the bridge until the fog bank is lifted.

Overview
This activity is very effective early in the school year. It teaches communication skills as well as sensitivity to the perspectives of others. It also creates an awareness of cultural diversity and an appreciation of new ideas. It allows students the oppor-

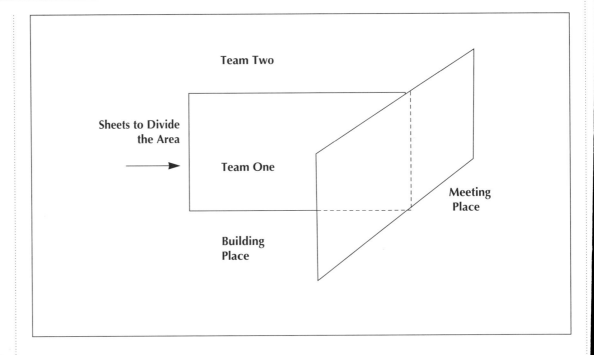

tunity to laugh, create and play while learning that cultural and linguistic differences can contribute to misunderstandings. It also emphasizes the need for compromise. The activity can be adapted for specific cultural traits and lessons. Cultural Bridge works best when used with small groups, i.e., four to six members.

Description
The object of the activity is

to build a bridge which is identical on each side of the "fog bank" (a sheet dividing the two teams).

STORY:
A team of Americans would like access to a very valuable energy resource available on a small Pacific island. The islanders have little use for this resource and are willing to help, but have little to gain from the deal so are relatively ambivalent about the whole

thing. Each group is given a sheet of paper with the following information:

ISLAND TEAM
You live in a simple culture on a small island near Hawaii which has only recently been discovered by the United States. Lying all over your beaches, and of no use to your people, is this special energy resource the United States explorers can iuse in their country. Since you have no use in for this

110

Teaching Notes:

stuff that is cluttering your beaches, and it can be removed with relatively little impact on your people or environment, you don't mind their taking it, but you have little to gain from the deal, so you aren't especially enthusiastic either. Your culture has a few unique characteristics that distinguish your people from the Americans. You are very polite people, signaling the conclusion of each statement with "thank you," which is then an invitation for response by those with whom you are talking. Islanders like to stand very close when speaking, almost toe to toe. This signals your respect and honesty to those with whom you speak. Islanders don't like to rush into business-like talk. Instead, all work-related meetings begin with the essential "water ceremony" during which participants make small talk while slowly sipping water from the traditional Dixie cups. When the ceremony is finished (and you've had enough water), you can get on to business. Lastly, you speak a dialect of English

with a few minor differences. Instead of saying: high, you say wide; egg carton, boat; top, bottom; and for one you stick out your tongue; two, pull on your right ear.

The objective of this exercise for the United States team, who want access to this resource on your island, is for both teams to build identical structures which meet when the fog lifts. If they are culturally sensitive and properly respectful, feel free to help them reach this goal. If you are offended, don't feel compelled to be too helpful. You will begin by having five minutes to build, then seven minutes to meet with United States representatives to discuss your plans, five more minutes to build more or modify your bridge, seven more minutes to meet, another building period, one more meeting, and one final building period. After these last modifications of your structure, the fog bank will lift and, we hope, your bridges will meet as a tribute to international cooperation.

UNITED STATES TEAM
A valuable source of an important energy resource has been found on a small island near Hawaii. You are representatives from the United States who have been sent to negotiate with the islanders to build a bridge connecting their island with Hawaii. They are willing, although not especially enthusiastic about giving you access to this resource for which they have no use. You know little about this island culture except that you both have the same resources for building this bridge, which must be identical on both sides of the "fog bank" currently separating the islands. You will have five minutes to build initially, then seven minutes to meet with island representatives to discuss your plans, five more minutes to build more or modify your bridge, seven more minutes to meet, another building period, one more meeting, and one final building period. After these last modifications of your structure, the fog bank will lift and, we hope, your bridge will meet with the

islanders giving you access to this important resource.

Rules
No peeking at the other team's structure. Meetings should be between one representative of each team, although teammates can help clarify things, give hints, etc. Representatives should be different for each meeting so that most participants are included.

Coaching from the teacher, especially before the first meeting, helps get the groups involved in the whole exercise.

Debriefing Questions
• Consider cultural differences, cultural cues, judgmental attitudes, cooperation and compromise, cultural values, sensitivity to the perspectives of others, diplomacy and if appropriate, gender/race/ethnicity roles.

Classroom Application
• Geography
• Social Studies
• History
• Politics

Initiatives

Point "A" To Point "B"

Contributed by: Sterling Catkey, Voyageur Outward Bound School

What's Learned
• Teamwork

Equipment
• Markers, sticks, flags, string etc.

Pre-activity Preparation
Mark a starting point (A) and ending point (B) approximately 20' to 25' apart. The area between the points should be level and free from obstructions.

Overview
This activity underscores the importance of cooperation and listening. If the group does not work as a team, the activity cannot be completed. It also brings people in touch with each other and creates a feeling of closeness.

Activity Introduction
Before the group is a swamp full of swamp critters. If the group crosses the swamp in 10 moves the swamp critters

will not be disturbed and the group can go on its way in safety.

Description
The group (no more than 5 people) must move together from Point A to Point B within 10 group moves. Each person's step counts as one move. Group sizes greater than five can be divided into two or more groups. A variation is to have the groups compete with each other.

Rules
The group is allowed five minutes for planning. They cannot speak to each other after the planning period has ended.

Solution
The group must band together and create human wheelbarrows to carry other members to complete the task within 10 moves.

Debriefing Questions
• What obstacles did the group encounter while planning the 10 moves?
• Was everyone willing to cooperate?
• What were the different leadership styles?
• How did individuals react to frustration?
• What allowed the activity to succeed?

Classroom Application
• Creating an idea
• Implementation

ACADEMIC STUDIES

In this chapter you will find a variety of mini-lessons. They are divided into four units, Unit I: Class Climate and Culture, Unit II: Natural Worlds, Unit III: Our Town, and Unit IV: Language Arts. These lessons are examples of activities for teachers to use with students in their classrooms. The format may vary between mini-lessons.

These mini-lessons represent an exploration by teachers of experiential strategies for the study of academic material and the personal growth that accompanies learning and maturation. Irrespective of the subject or content of each mini-lesson, the context and process that guide student and teacher conduct are rooted in the previously discussed pedagogies and principles of Outward Bound. Thus whether one is studying environmental sciences or sociology, student and teacher alike will find themselves immersed in experience, challenged by the dynamic interplay of teamwork and individual effort, served by communication skills learned, guided by compassion, afforded opportunities for self-examination and reflection, and immersed in study and activity that calls forth their very best.

CHAPTER 8

Unit I: Class Climate and Culture

. . . knowledge of truth alone does not suffice; on the contrary . . . knowledge must continually be renewed by ceaseless effort, if it is not to be lost. It resembles a statue of marble which stands in the desert and is continuously threatened with burial by the shifting sand. The hands of service must ever be at work . . .

—Albert Einstein

The purpose of this unit is to present lessons that will introduce students to the major concepts of Outward Bound pedagogies and philosophy, as well as general active-learning principles.

Regardless of the academic focus of the class, to establish the context of active learning, group development initiatives should be used extensively during this phase. Activities that complement reading and writing will be introduced to explore the major themes of leadership, responsibility, self-discovery, and communication. Basic class procedures will also be introduced: Rotating Leadership, Journalizing, Celebration, Circle up, Briefing, Debriefing and Holistic Engagement.

During all units, consider:

- the interdisciplinary nature of activities.

- using experience to amplify learning.

- using multi-age and multi-ability groupings.

- having students apply their knowledge to real-life challenges facing individuals, the school-community or the community at large.

- creating linkages to other classes and other entities beyond the school, such as local, state, or federal agencies, businesses, or other organizations.

Teaching Notes:

First Contact

Contributed by: Mitchell Sakofs, Outward Bound Inc.

Grade Level
• All grades

Subject
• All subjects

Duration
• Two or more class periods

Objective
• To present ideas on group process, teamwork and communication and provide opportunities for participants to explore their own style in group activities.

Procedures
Circle Up and explain that:
• Insights into what makes a group work will better enable the students to evaluate and refine how they participate in activities.
• They will be engaged in activities that will help them learn about group process, teamwork and communications.
• Everyone will have a

chance to participate and reflect on associated issues through discussion and writing.
• Lead several activities using the brief-activity-debrief sequence. Begin with an initiative that requires a minimum amount of trust, such as a Group Juggle or a Name Game. Sequence events to lead to greater trust and communication. Debrief after every activity. Some additional initiatives

might include Toxic River or Traffic Jam. Building trust-based relationships between classmates will require careful planning. Do not rush into activities that require too much touching and make sure the students are physically and emotionally able to do the activities.
• Provide a conceptual framework for understanding group work, introduce basic concepts such as active listening,

task-oriented gate keeping or blocking behaviors, as well as the stages of group formation (forming, storming, norming and performing).
• Reflect on group process and encourage reflection toward self-discovery and learning new, effective personal skills.
• Introduce additional activities.

Teaching Notes:

BIOGRAPHIES

Contributed by:
Mitchell Sakofs,
Outward Bound, Inc.

Grade Level
• Middle and High School

Subject
• All subjects

Duration
• 1 to 2 class periods

Objective
• To help create a climate of trust and assist students to reflect on what qualities they and class-members bring to the group.

Materials
• Paper and writing instruments.

Procedures
• Circle up and: A) Explain the value of knowing each other in building respect, trust and appreciation.B) Give examples of interesting aspects of certain people's lives whom all the students know, such as, students who have lived overseas or who have interesting hobbies, or teachers, administrators and others who have interesting stories and skills. C) Ask group members if any of them has ever skied, rock climbed, visited or lived in other countries. (Consciously try to show everyone that everyone has something unique and interesting about them.) This can take 10 minutes or an entire class period. Use your judgment.

• When you are ready to move to the next phase, have class members pair up and interview each other with the expressed purpose of developing a fairly comprehensive biography. Suggest such questions as Where were you born? What are your favorite television shows or books? Get information about parents, grandparents, pets, interests, and/or sports.

• Once both members of the pair have had a chance to interview each other, they should each develop a biography of the other. Developing the Biography should have several phases (see page 148 for writing process.) During the formative phases of the biography, provide time for the pairs to get together so that individuals can share their stories and seek refinements from their counterparts.

• As a conclusion to this activity, authors can introduce their subjects during class, and students can, if they so choose, ask questions to learn about their classmates.

Extensions
• This assignment can be expanded to create a play about class members.

• Assignments can also be bound into a Who's Who volume.

• Extending the assignment beyond the class, the class can take on additional projects to develop biographies of all the faculty and staff in a school and develop a Who's Who compendium for a school; likewise such a compendium can be developed for an entire grade.

Unit I

Teaching Notes:

Leadership Sequencing

Contributed By: Mitchell Sakofs, Outward Bound Inc.

Grade Level
• Middle or High School

Subject
• All subjects

Duration
• Two or more class periods

Objectives
• To present ideas on the theory and practice of leadership.
• To provide opportunities for students to reflect on issues of leadership, leadership models, styles and skills, and to have students explore their own leadership styles in action.

Materials
• As defined by specific initiatives or projects

Procedures
• Circle up and explain that:
  A) Insights into what makes a good leader will better enable the students

to evaluate and refine their own leadership skills.
B) They will be engaged in

activities that will help them learn about leadership. C) Everyone will

have a chance to lead and follow and to reflect upon leadership practice through discussion and in writing.
• Lead several activities using brief-activity-debrief sequence.
• Introduce basic leadership concepts, such as, laissez faire, democratic, autocratic and situational, to provide a conceptual framework for understanding leadership.
• Continue with activities, by having different students lead the brief-activity-debrief process.
• Reflect on group process as well as leadership.

Extension
Build on the students' experience as leaders to explore the role of a leader within a community. Classes can organize to research the concept by interviewing various community leaders (e.g., religious, governmental, law enforcement, or school), to gain insight into motivations, styles, and other areas of interest.

CHAPTER 9

Unit II: The Natural World

What is life: It is the flash of a firefly in the night.
It is the breath of a buffalo in the winter;
it is the little shadow which runs across the grass
and loses itself in the sunset.

— Crowfoot

Introduction

This unit introduces lessons to enhance a student's understanding and appreciation of the natural world, while also teaching scientific content and skills integral to the scientific method.

This section is rooted in two key perspectives: 1) humanity requires raw materials and a healthy environment in order to survive and 2) given the scope, nature and impact of human activity on world ecology, an understanding of the natural world is essential to creating and sustaining a healthy environment.

To achieve the objectives of this section, lessons will focus on field investigations, readings, lectures, and trips. Students will choose projects that will enable them to focus on the natural environment. Some projects that might be explored include the keeping of phenological notes; plant and animal life inventories; or working with local, state and/or federal officials in environmental protection, or fish and wildlife agencies. To launch this unit, survey the resources within your community, such as, local, state and federal agencies concerned with the environment; or local museums, clubs, organizations as well as businesses. Some of the less obvious resources include waste disposal companies, utilities, and land developers. Either through field trips or in-class presenters, have representatives from these various agencies come and present to your class. In preparation for these presentations, student groups should undertake research projects designed to identify substantive issues relative to the topic of discussion. Likewise, students can pursue information on the companies the presenters represent, such as, what issues they are currently concerned with or litigation they may be involved in.

Teaching Notes:

FIELD INVESTIGATION

Contributed By: Deb Eads, The Eagle Rock School,Estes Park, Colorado, (Colorado Outward Bound School)

Grade level
• Grades seven to nine

Subject
• Science, Language Arts

Duration
• One class period

Objective
• To learn the techniques of observation and measurement of plant and animal life in a designated area.

Materials
Each student will need an investigation sheet, pencil, cardboard backing, ruler, hand lens, string, and tape (to tape hands).

Procedures
Each student will mark off a section of the field with string to designate boundaries. A ruler and a hand lens should also be issued to

each student. Each student will have a forestry wheel (investigation sheet) to complete.

Students divide into teams of three. Allow 20-30 minutes for each team of students to explore their areas. (Areas are selected by the students and defined by the string).

Students make observations, take measurements and complete the investigation sheet at different levels. (They complete a sheet about what they observe at the surface, a sheet about what they observe at one inch down and another at

three inches down).

When the time is up, gather all the teams together and compare findings. Especially note the differences between opposite environments—shady and sunny spots, moist and dry areas, mowed lawns and unmoved fields.

Each student should then "rebuild" his plot until it looks as though he had not been there.

Before taking the class outside, it is a good idea to discuss the investigation sheet indoors and give examples of what the different students may find. This

helps to structure the activity so that students have a better idea of what is expected of them.

The field investigation sheet can be modified to suit the needs of almost any lesson plan. It can be used in the study of plants or animals in the ponds, streams, fields or forests. The investigation can be of one area in particular, or can compare different sites or habitats. You can make up your own investigation sheet to study physical properties, for instance, different layers of soil, or different bodies of water.

Extensions
Have the students write essays about what they observed in their plots.

Discuss with students how different it felt exploring with their hands taped and using only their thumb and first finger. Discuss how life might be different if we only could use those two fingers.

Discuss what life might be like for those who are handicapped and have only partial mobility in their hands.

Teaching Notes:

PEBBLE/STICK GAME

Contributed By: Deb Eads, The Eagle Rock School, Estes Park, Colorado, (Colorado Outward Bound School)

Grade level
• Grades seven to nine

Subject
• Science

Duration
• One class period

Objective
• To use the students' sense of touch to observe an object closely and later to distinguish it from others.

Materials
• Each student picks up her own unique stick (rock).

Procedures
Each student may pick up a stick (rock) then carefully investigate her own stick (rock) for about two minutes.

Students should note:
– What shape is it?
– How big is it compared to her hand?

– Is it warm or cool?
– Is it moist or dry?

The teacher then collects the sticks (rocks), mixes them together and then hands them out to students behind their backs.

Students then try to find their original sticks (rock) by passing them around in a circle, behind their backs. When the student finds her stick (rock) she holds on to it.

Extensions
Try this activity with different kinds of leaves (or even leaves from the same tree), cones, nuts or any other common objects found outside.

Emphasize the variety that lies hidden in nature and how students can see this variety if they look closely.

Teaching Notes:

EYE SEE

Contributed by: Deb Eads, The Eagle Rock School, Estes Park, Colorado, (Colorado Outward Bound School)

Grade Level
• All

Subject
• Science

Duration
• One class period

Objective
• To develop a heightened awareness of the sense of sight and to increase the ability to notice small details.

Materials
• None

Procedure
Have the group break up into pairs and face each other. Direct students to carefully observe their partners. After a set time, signal the pairs to turn away in place and stand back to back. Each participant then changes something visible on herself, such as pushing up a sleeve or taking off an earring. With another signal, the partners again face each other and attempt to spot the changes. Repeat activity as many times as desired.

Debrief
Were you able to spot changes in your partner?

What can you do to improve your powers of observation?

Did you observe things other than the physical (e.g., how your partner was feeling?)

Why is it important to "see well"?

What are typical ways to look at change?

Are there other ways to create change?

What animals can you think of that rely upon their sight the most?

Discuss with students how much of our world we never really "see."

Teaching Notes:

Lilliput Trails

Contributed By: Mitchell Sakofs, Outward Bound Inc.

Grade level
• Middle and High School

Subjects
• Science — Field Natural History

Duration
• One to two class periods

Objective
• To have the students use their knowledge of field natural history and powers of observation to lay out a miniature nature trail.

Materials
• 25' to 30' lengths of light string or cord for each member of the group.
• A limited number of magnifying glasses and blindfolds for use by students.

Procedures
Choose an area with a unique natural history. Distribute string and other equipment. Circle up and:

Define the area in which

the group may work. (Make it large enough so that students can find sufficient space to work and you can oversee and manage activities.)

Explain that they are each to select an area of interest and lay out a miniature nature trail to be defined by the string. The trail should have various stations illustrating interesting features of the area and natural processes.

Each trail should have between 10 and 15 stations.

The trail can range along the ground, or up into trees or bushes.

Students should be prepared to lead a fellow classmate through the trail.

Remind students to take care not to have a negative impact on the area in which they are working.

Students should have sufficient time for each to lay out his trail, pair up with another student, and lead his partner on the trail he constructed.

Circle up and debrief.

Extensions
Students can be encouraged to think about feelings associated with stations, and if time allows, to draw or write reactions or thoughts.

If the property allows for it, these initial field studies can be used to identify potential sites for the development of a nature trail or potential service projects.

Into The Classroom:

Teaching Notes:

Revelations

Contributed By: Mitchell Sakofs, Outward Bound Inc.

Grade Level
• Middle and High School

Subject
• Science

Duration
• One class period

Objective
• To provide an opportunity for students to experience solitude and allow the natural world to reveal itself to the students.

Materials
• None

Procedures
Bring students to an area of unique natural beauty; a local nature center, for example. Circle up and explain that:

• When people enter an area, the noises and smells associated with their presence often cause the animal life to move into hiding;

• In order to create an opportunity for the animal life to reveal itself to the students, they must move into the forest and find a place to sit alone, absolutely still and silent;

• Once they've found their place, they are to sit and remain as still and silent as possible– for 20 minutes to a half an hour;

• In their silence, they should be alert for sounds, smells and sights of the forest habituating to their presence and the increase in animal life activity.

• In addition, introduce the "sound" that you will make in order to call them back together. (I suggest clapping your hands.)

• Define the boundaries of the area clearly.

•Send them off when you are ready.

• After calling the group back together, circle up and discuss their experiences. Allow conversation to address observations of nature as well as thoughts and feelings that might have emerged.

Extensions
This project can lead to assignments in journal writing.

Teaching Notes:

Forest Ecology Study

Contributed by Scott Hartl, Expeditionary Learning Outward Bound

Grade level
• Tenth grade

Subject
• Biology

Duration
• Three weeks

Objectives
• To utilize a hands-on approach to learning in which students interact with the natural world.
• To reinforce students' understanding of methods of biological research and use of natural history journals.
• To explore the relationship between habitat and species composition.
• To integrate writing as an important part of the scientific process.

Material
Plant press, water-testing kit, blindfolds, stakes and line for transect study, ropes and hardware for rappel, tree-coring tool, binoculars and field journals.

Procedures
Pre-trip activities:
• Introduction to tree life cycles, structure and identification.
• Introduction to the early spring plants, structure and identification.
• Student research, written report and oral presentation on the lifecycle of one local indigenous organism.

Field Trip Activities:
• Guided natural history tour of local forest.
• Students must generate 20 or more questions about things that intrigued them during the tour.
• Blindfolded tree identification exercise.
• Transect study of a selected site. The transect will be two feet. wide and approximately 50 feet long and cut through more than one habitat. This transect will be divided into study plots, each worked by two students. All plants will be described in student journals, entered onto data collection sheets, and collected for pressing.
• Time for research and observation of each student's specialty species.
• Several representative trees will be cored for dendrochronology sample. (Permission must be obtained for this).

Follow-up activities:
Students will take the list of 20 questions generated during the guided natural history tour. They will choose their five favorites and, for each, generate two hypotheses which might answer the question. A group discussion will follow to share questions and discuss possible answers. Each student will then choose his or her favorite question, research the answer and write a short report.

Students should prepare a report of the transect study. Research methods of the study will be documented, data for species composition will be compiled using the Cricket Graph, plant samples will be dried and presented, pictures will be mounted with captions, and the biological significance discussed.

Supplement the life-cycle reports of each student's specialty species with their observations and research from the field.

Evaluation
Students will receive grades on the following portions of this project:

• Written life-cycle report.
• Oral presentation of life-cycle report
• Field journal
• Transect report
• A short paper researching their chosen natural history question (from the list of questions that they generated during the guided natural history tour.)
• Final product: Written report, in scientific paper format (introduction, methods, results, discussion), of the transect study to be conducted during the field day. Pressed samples of common plants and pictures to be included. Results of water chemistry testing and its significance will be compiled using the Cricket Graph.

Unit II

CHAPTER 10

Unit III: Our Town

I don't know what your destiny will be,
but one thing I know: the only ones among you
who will be really happy are those who will have
sought and found how to serve.

— Albert Schweitzer

Introduction

Most towns are a rich mosaic of people with countless interests, cultures and values. These dimensions of a town constitute central themes that bring people together into communities and also serve as barriers that alienate communities from each other.

To contribute to a social climate that honors people, understanding communities is essential. This unit presents lessons for you to use with your students to help them explore and better understand the various ethnic, religious, economic and professional communities that exist within their cities and towns.

The lessons suggest active community explorations, community service, interviews, readings, films and guest lecturers as the means by which students will come to understand the multifaceted nature of their communities. Through learning about their community, students can come to an understanding of ways to work with the community members to address exciting problems. Students at all grade levels can learn a lot through helping others and reflecting on the process.

Unit III

Special thanks to Trina Abbott, Coordinator of Special Projects, Outward Bound, Inc., for helping with this unit.

Teaching Notes:

Community Study

Contributed by: Susan McCray, New York City Outward Bound

Grade level
• High School

Subject
• Social Science

Duration
• Seven to eight class periods

Objective
• To provide an opportunity for students to understand their community.

Materials
• Maps, newspaper articles, and books. Plan ahead and schedule meetings with leaders in the community.

Procedures
Day One
Define the image: Set the scene by having your students imagine they come from a far-off planet. (Give it a name.) Tell them they have just landed in town, and have them write a description of the town from the perspective of an extraterrestrial visitor.

Have the students read their stories. And as they read, create two lists on the board: 1) Truths and 2) Stories, Myths and Exaggerations. Discuss the meaning of these terms and as items go on the board, encourage discussion to refine understandings about the town.

Homework: Find at least one newspaper article that describes some aspect of life in your town.

Day Two
Have students read articles out loud. Discuss how the images presented in the articles relate to the lists developed the previous day and contribute to people's opinions about the community. Are they positive? Negative? Accurate?

Days Three & Five
Divide the class into small groups and have group members identify major themes appearing in the news about their town.

Create a master list of major themes and then have each group select one theme that is of most interest to them in exploring. Groups should undertake a research effort to understand that issue. Their objective will be to present the scope and nature of the issue they selected along with major themes, positions, et cetera, to the rest of the class.

Day Six & Seven
Groups present the results of their research and discussion is permitted.

Teaching Notes:

Community-based Research

Contributed By: Jim Austin & Jerry Towsend, Cooperstown, New York, Middle and High Schools

Grade Level
• High School

Subject
• Social Science

Duration
• Ten class periods

Objective
• To provide an opportunity for students to explore and understand their community and engage in meaningful community service.

Materials
• Maps, newspaper articles, and books. Plan ahead and schedule meetings with leaders from the community

Procedures

Days One and Two
Using a consensus decision-making process, the group should select one issue for in-depth community-based study. Specific issues should be identified relative to the issue and tasks related to researching and documenting the effort should be identified.

In preparation for this study the class should organize itself into task-groups and develop a coordinated group structure to plan a community study.

Day Three to Five
Strategies for gathering essential information should be developed in small groups.

Small groups should present their ideas to the larger group for comment and feedback.

Small groups should take the information provided to them to restructure their community investigations.

Days Six and Seven
Groups execute their plans.

Days Eight & Nine
Groups analyze data and develop reports for class.

Days Ten & Eleven
• Group reports.

Extensions
If the research and perspectives gathered by the students can contribute intelligently to the debate around the issues researched, their work should be polished for presentation to community leaders.

If appropriate, students can undertake an initiative to utilize their research to offer service to their community. Examples of services school groups have provided to the community include: EMT support, consumer goods recycling, peer counseling, and park reclamation.

Unit III

Teaching Notes:

Mathematics Measurements Straight Lines

Contributed By:
George P. Armstrong,
Thompson Island Outward Bound Center

Grade Level
• Middle School

Subject
• Mathematics

Duration
• Three to four class periods with homework

Objectives
During this activity the student will:
• Make a "ground measuring tool."
• Use the tool to determine distances.
• Become aware of the difference between an estimated distance based on sight and the actual distance based on computations.

Materials
• Pencil, notebook or paper, tin can, tape measure, pocket knife, clothes, hanger and paint.

Procedures

TASK I – Selecting Materials
Using a tape measure, find:

1. A tin can that measures approximately 12" in circumference.
2. Two, 4' sticks, about 1-1/2 - 2" in diameter.
3. One flat and fairly straight 1" x 2" or 1" x 1" or 2" x 2" board that measures at least 30" long. (If a board is not available, a straight stick of about 1-1/2" diameter and 30" long can be used).
4 You will also need a pocket knife and a small amount of paint (no more than 1/4 pint).

TASK II – Constructing A Measuring Tool:

Using the materials from the first task, you will now construct the following measuring tools:

1. Take the 12" circumference tin can and paint a single straight line about 1/2" wide from the top of the can to the bottom. Allow the paint to dry.
2. Using your knife, punch a small hole in the center of each end of the can. Holes should not be larger than 3/8".
3. Take the wire coat hanger and straighten it out. Then insert the straightened wire through the can using the holes you created.
4. Cut a 1" deep slot in each of the two 4' sticks. Insert wire in the slots on the sticks to complete your measuring instrument.

Now you can measure distance in feet by pushing the can on the ground in front of you, or pulling it behind you and counting each time you see the painted line at the top of the revolving can.

TASK III – Comparing Estimated Distance With Measured Distance:

Find a relatively level terrain area such as a field or opening in the woods. Find a fixed point (a tree, rock or hill) and guess how far it is from where you are standing. Indicate your guess in feet and mark it in your notebook. Now pace off the distance by walking with long steps. Based on the fact that each step is considered to be approximately three feet, multiply the number of steps by three to get another estimate of the distance. Record this in your notebook. Now, using your "ground measuring tool," measure the actual distance and record the results in your notebook. Remember, each revolution of the tin can is equal to one foot. Compare your figures. Is there much difference in the three measurements? Which estimated measurement (sight or pacing) is closest to the true measurement? Write these observations in your notebook.

TASK IV – Student Assignments

Measure three city or town blocks and record their measurements on page 135.

Teaching Notes:

City or Town _____ Date _____

Street Names on all four sides	Measurement of each side (in ft.)	Total feet in the block (perimeter)
1. _____	_____	_____
2. _____	_____	_____
3 _____	_____	_____
4. _____	_____	_____

City or Town _____ Date _____

Street Names on all four sides	Measurement of each side (in ft.)	Total feet in the block (perimeter)
1. _____	_____	_____
2. _____	_____	_____
3 _____	_____	_____
4. _____	_____	_____

City or Town _____ Date _____

Street Names on all four sides	Measurement of each side (in ft.)	Total feet in the block (perimeter)
1. _____	_____	_____
2. _____	_____	_____
3 _____	_____	_____
4. _____	_____	_____

- Measure the distance from your home to the following and record the distances below:

Home address: _____

Location	Distance in Feet
1. Post Office	1. _____
2. City Hall	2. _____
3. School	3. _____
4. Library	4. _____

- You will measure the distance in feet from your home to the home of your best friend. Write the distance below:

Distance in feet to the house of:

NAME:_____

ADDRESS:_____

DISTANCE:_____

Now convert the distance in feet to distance in inches. (12 inches to each foot)

INCHES: _____

Unit III

Into The Classroom:

Service Internship

Contributed By: Scott Hartl, Expeditionary Learning Outward Bound.

Grade Level
• High school

Subject
• Social studies

Duration
• Optional

Objective
• To inspire students to get involved in their communities.
• To help the students gain a better understanding of their community and its needs.

Materials
• Basic information Form
• Interview Form

Procedures
Setting up your internship: Identify a service organization in the city that you feel does important work. This organization should be easily accessible by foot, bus, car, etc. The type of work

the organization does should be of strong personal interest to you. Contact this organization and ask if they

are able to take volunteers. The organization must be able to provide you with supervision and any neces-

sary training. When you find an organization that meets those criteria then fill out the basic information form and get approval from the teacher. You then need to set up a work schedule for between ten and twenty hours in a predetermined time-frame.

Journal
Keep a journal that documents your experiences while working. For each time that you work you need to describe what you spent your time doing, your thoughts and feelings concerning the experience, and any interesting stories from the day. Your journal entries should be written within a day of working so that details will be fresh and full. The journal will be turned in to the teacher after five hours of work and then again when your hours are completed. Possible questions to address in your journal include:

• What did you do?
• What interesting thing happened?
• Describe the people that you worked with.

Teaching Notes:

- Describe one person whom you thought was particularly interesting.
- Describe your supervisor:
  - How did she or he treat you, and what did you think of her or him?
- Describe the other people you worked with. How did they treat you and what did you think of them?
- How did the kids respond to you?
- What was the building like where you worked?
- What was the equipment like where you worked?
- What do you think of this organization?
- What is it like working for no pay?
- What did you learn today?
- What are you gaining from this experience?

Interview

During your first or second visit you need to set up a short interview with your supervisor. This interview is aimed at providing you with some basic background information about the organization with which you are working. The interview can be tape recorded and transcribed onto the interview

form and them turned in to the teacher.

Final paper

To bring closure to this project the student will write a paper based on three resources: an interview with the supervisor, journal entries, and personal experience. The report paper needs to address the following topics:

- What services does the organization provide for the community?
- What problems does the organization face in its attempt to provide these services successfully?
- How effective is the organization in providing these services?
- What are one or two suggestions you have for how this organization could become more effective in providing its services. Be specific and present the rationale behind your suggestion(s).
- What did you learn from the time you spent working with this organization?

Basic Information Form

Name of organization:

Phone number:

Location of organization:

Name of possible supervisor:

....

Interview Form

How do you plan to get there?

Why have you chosen this organization?

What services does this organization provide for the community?

How old is this organization?

What is the annual budget (approximately)?

What are the biggest problems faced by this organization?

What are some of this organization's goals for the coming years?

Unit III

Teaching Notes:

Social History Cemetery Study

Contributed by:
George P. Armstrong,
Thompson Island Outward Bound Center

Grade level
• Middle and High School

Subject
• Social Studies

Duration
• Five class periods

Objectives
In this activity you will gather data from the historical record as recorded on cemetery markers. This will provide you with an historical snapshot of community life from one generation to the next.

• Collect information from grave markers.
• Use the collected information to show historical and environmental patterns and events.
• Discuss the implications of your findings.

Materials
• Paper and pencils

Procedures
First Task – Data Collecting:

Student Assignment – Locate a community cemetery and complete Data Sheet 1 and II. Be sure to secure permission to visit the site. Discuss your cemetery selection with other members of your class so you do not all go to the same areas. You can work in teams to collect the information trying to cover as many cemeteries within the community as the class can .

On your Data Sheet 1 is a section for notes. In this section you should try to determine the answers to the following questions:

• What nationalities do the names suggest?
• Can family size be determined?
• Can patterns of in-or-out migration be determined?
• Are there any unmarked graves? What might explain the unmarked graves? (Use the back of the Data Sheet if you need more room.)

• If an inscription appears on the marker, record the inscription on Data Sheet 2.

Student Note:- On markers that are hard to read due to weathering you can make rubbings using rice paper or school manila paper and a large wax crayon to bring out the differences between raised and cut surfaces. (See Data Sheet No.1 in the appendices of this book.)

Second Task – Processing the Collected Information:

Student Assignment I – After you have collected the information on Data Sheet 1 and II, reconstruct this information on the individual graph sheets.

Student Assignment II - After completing your individual graphs your teacher will furnish the class with a master graph for collating information on a total community scale. (See Data Sheet No.2 in the appendices of this book.)

Third Task – Conclusions:

Student Assignment – After completing the master graph, formulate some answers to the following questions. (Refer back to your Data Sheets, individual graphs and the class masters.)

Disscussion: Self-Image
How can we tell from your information what people thought of themselves? What their relatives thought of them? (Clues: inscription, marker, marker size)

Discussion: Family Life
What does your data indicate about family size? Does family size decline over the decades? When do inscriptions in various foreign languages first appear? When do they completely cease? Is there evidence that one national group was socially dominant? What is it? How can you tell?

Discussion: State of Medicine and Health Care
What does your data on age of death and cause of death indicate about medical care in former decades? What

Teaching Notes:

evidence is there of epidemics? Do the epidemics appear to be seasonal?

Discussion: Historical Events
Is there evidence of local historical events: fires,

World War II, Indian wars or battles, Korean War, Floods, War in Viet Nam, Civil War, World War I, town fires,

earthquakes, natural disasters or other significiant events?

Into The Classroom:

Teaching Notes:

Data Sheet No. 1

Name	Birth	Death	Marker	Type	Notes

Marker: (granite, limestone, sandstone, wood, ect.)
Type: (slab, post, block, ect.)
Notes: (Veteran, death at childbirth, religion, cause of death)

Teaching Notes:

Data Sheet No. 2

Name   **Inscription of Deceased**

Teaching Notes:

Deaths by Year

Years	Count	Birth	Death	Marker	Notes
1990-+					
1980/89					
1970/79					
1960/69					
1950/59					
1940/49					
1930/39					
1920/29					
1910/19					
1900/09					
1890/99					
1880/89					
1870/79					
Before 1869					

Year
(Intervals of Ten Years)

Teaching Notes:

Deaths by Month of Year

Month	Count	Death Date	Marker	Notes
Jan				
Feb				
Mar				
April				
May				
June				
July				
Aug				
Sept				
Oct				
Nov				
Dec				
No Month				

Optional: Male (blue dot), Female (red dot)

Unit III

Teaching Notes:

Deaths by Age, Sex and Years

Male (blue dot)
Female (red dot)

	Male	Female	0-10 yrs.	11-19 yrs.	(Ect.)...
1990 (-/+)					
1980/89					
1970/79					
1960/69					
1950/59					
1940/49					
1930/39					
1920/29					
1910/19					
1900/09					
1890/99					
1880/89					
1870/79					
Before 1869					

Year
(Intervals of Ten years)

Marker Type

(Number of Markers)

Color Code: Red, Blue, Black, Green, Orange
Marker Type: Block w/square top, Block w/round top, etc.

1990 (-/+)	
1980/89	
1970/79	
1960/69	
1950/59	
1940/49	
1930/39	
1920/29	
1910/19	
1900/09	
1890/99	
1880/89	
1870/79	
Before 1869	

Year
(Intervals of 10 years)

Teaching Notes:

Community Service

Contributed by: Trina Abbott, Coordinator of Special Projects, Outward Bound, Inc.

Grade level
• All grades

Subject
• Social Science

Duration
• Determined by individual project

Objective
• To engage students in community service.

• To assist students in translating service to service learning.

Materials
• A Community-based Research Study (see page 127)
• A journal.

Procedures
In creating a community service project, students need to involve the community and do service for the community that is appreciated and needed. Students should:

• Conduct a Community-based research study as described in the previous pages.

• Identify one or more community service projects and present ideas to community members. If community members are willing to work with you to make the project happen, then it is a good one.
• Let community members know what you are doing and ask them to join you, if appropriate.
• Do the community service project—this may be a one day event or an ongoing year long/multi-year project.
• Reflect on the experience through journal writing and discussion.

Ideas
Suggestion for community service projects are:

• Address and environmental problem by rehabilitating parks, vacant lots, hiking and walking trails or organize a recycling and trash pick-up event.
• Address human concerns through setting up visiting residents in a nursing home or VA hospital.
• Address educational needs through a class project that involves younger and older students learning from each other.
• Address public safety needs through assisting police in community watches, educating community members in basic first aid and responding to emergencies.

Service Learning
Learning through service comes from reflecting and discussion of service activities. After a day of service, whether a single day event or an on-going project, students can reflect by writing a journal. Question could model: What did you do today? Who at your service site did you interact with? What did you learn form them? What, if any, would you like to do differently next time you go to the site?

Discussions are a great way to share journal entries and discuss the following ideas: Why is the service I am doing important? Is it solving a problem? If not, how can we solve the problem? What will I do in the future to give back to my community?

CHAPTER 11

Unit IV: Language Arts

I hate quotations. Tell me what you know..

— R. W. Emerson

Introduction

In the active learning classroom we use powerful real-life and simulated experiences that generate emotion as a springboard to learn and improve skills in reading and written and verbal combination.

Teaching Notes:

Experience Based Writing Approach

Contributed By: Flo Levin, North Carolina Outward Bound School

Grade level
• Middle and High School

Subject
• English

Duration
• Two to three class periods

Objectives
• To increase the student's understanding and enjoyment of written and spoken English.

• To improve specific skills in writing, reading, verbal expression and vocabulary.

Procedures
The Language Experience Approach consists of the following stages:

• **Prewrite:** This stage provides the subject matter.

It involves participation in an experience such as rock climbing, a day hike or working in a homeless shelter. Upon completing the experience the teachers helps the students to rethink the experience and start writing. This is accomplished through discussion, brainstorming key words or ideas, and reinforcing vocabulary.

• **Freewrite**: During this stage students are encouraged to write freely, without concern for form, grammar, or mechanics. They write anything that comes to mind regarding their experience. Ideally, the Freewrite phase immediately follows Prewrite discussions and should be limited to about 20 minutes.

• **Write**: The students set to the task of culling through Freewrite material, deleting, substituting and rearranging ideas. During this stage the central idea of the writing is developed but it is still considered to be in a formative stage.

• **Rewrite:** During this stage, the student is engaged in revising the product of the Write stage. The story and images are refined. Spelling is corrected by having the student look up words and feedback is provided by peers. During this stage the student and teacher meet for formal discussion around format, style and structure. The writing sample is explored word by word, line by line.

• **Polish**: During this phase the focus is on detail: correct capitalization, punctuation, spelling and grammar. When completed, the work is in its final form, neat and error free.

• **Publish:** The student work is displayed on bulletin boards, read in public, taken home and published in-house.

Activity
Any activity that evokes strong emotion is ripe for use with this writing process. In essence, the students will write if they have something to say. Powerful experiences create that desire. In Outward Bound such traditional experiences as technical rock climbing, camping, backpacking and canoeing have been used to create the emotional springboards for engaging in the writing process, but almost any of the experiences in this book can serve this purpose.

148

Teaching Notes:

Word Bank

Contributed by:
Flo Levin, North Carolina
Outward Bound School

Grade Level
• All grades

Subject
• Language Arts

Duration
• One class period

Objective
• To have students learn new vocabulary words.

Materials
• Poster paper (newsprint), masking tape, magic markers, and dictionaries.

Procedures
• Circle up and using a Socratic style of questioning, have your students talk about words. What are they? How are they used? Where do they come from? How do we learn them?

• Lead the discussion to special words the students know. As students offer words, write them on the newsprint, and ask students to spell and define them if they can.

• Build on their enthusiasm and solicit words they would like to share and deposit into a word bank for all to use.

* Keep it interactive and exciting.

• When they are through, tape the newsprint to the wall for their future reference and use. Encourage them to write them in their journals for safe keeping.

Extension
• Since this can be a regular part of the class, you may want to introduce a theme or topic at the beginning of a week and let them know that the word bank activity will be played on a certain day. This will give them time to search out new words that relate to that topic. (Encourage them to seek out new words through any and all means: books, newspapers, magazines, a dictionary, a thesaurus, conversations with people, et cetera).

• In keeping with the spirit of active learning, word themes should relate to an activity they will be engaging in. Remember, the more powerful and emotionally provocative the activity, the more excited and stimulated the students will be.

Teaching Notes:

POETRY

Contributed By:
George P. Armstrong,
Thompson Island Outward
Bound Center

Grade Level
• High School

Subject
• Literature

Duration
• Three to five class periods

Objectives
During this activity the student will:

• Take a field trip and identify various natural sights, hear and understand the meaning of sounds, and smell new smells.

• Learn to capture nature through writing about it in descriptive phrases.

• Learn to use descriptive adjectives to add life to the subject that is being written about.

• The student will use your descriptive phrases to compose two memorable poems:

– about your field trip
– about the emotions you feel during the field trip.

Procedures

TASK I - Field Trip
Find a secluded wooded area (preferably with a brook or stream) and with a notebook and pencil take a hike or leisurely stroll for about an hour. This will be done alone and without anything with you that would disturb your keen senses, i.e. radio, book or magazine, or food (including chewing gum).

As you stroll through the woods, you will:

• Observe the colors and various shades of colors, i.e., a green leaf with its silvery shades underneath, a sparrow and its many shades of brown and tan, a chipmunk and its autumn gold fur with black and white stripes.

• Stop every now and then and be as quiet as possible. Listen to the many sounds. Listen to the songs of the birds, the quick dashes of the chipmunks, squirrels and other animals; listen to a bird feeding, hear the pecking of a woodpecker; hear the soothing sounds of a brook or stream with its water curling around a smooth stone and the gentle rippling sound of the fast water. You can hear many new sounds when you listen quietly to the wind or breeze. Wind often has a musical sound with its whistling, rustling and whooshing sounds.

Now that the student has seen and heard the surroundings in the host environment, she or he will touch and smell many of the objects that have been observed. Smell and touch:

• flowers

• leaves

• dirt

• water

• the air (a breeze often carries the odors of

• flowers, leaves, moisture and decaying plant life)

TASK II
Now you will find a quiet and comfortable spot to sit while you put your pencil and notebook, as well as your deepest imagination, to work. You will pick one or two objects that you noticed during your hike and, using all your senses, i.e. sight, hearing, touch and smell, write descriptive phrases.

Take a tree as an example. Write various phrases using as many descriptive words as possible to describe it, its parts, and its surroundings. (Example: Phrase "wind swaying the trees"—finished line; "the North wind sways the trees preparing to strip their limbs."

Do you notice how we took a simple four word phrase and gave it life and meaning? We have not only told where the wind came from but have also established to the reader that fall is near and the limbs (branches) are getting ready to shed their leaves. Now let's take a look at the area around the tree and write

Teaching Notes:

about it. (Example: Phrase –"animals collecting food" Finished line – "Squirrels, chipmunks and winter birds collect food for the long months ahead.")

Now that we have established that it is fall, we can use our imagination as to what happens during this time of the year to a tree. What happens to a tree in the fall? ANSWER: The tree's sap drains downward and the leaves fall to the ground. The sap of the tree is like blood in a person. Rather than write about the sap, we could describe this happening as follows:

"Blood of the tree drains downward; soon life will give way to falling fingers."

It is important that we describe not only the object, but all of its surroundings, colors, feels, smells and climate. Notice how this has been done using the aforementioned phrases and finished lines in the accompanying poem,

Now, without copying the above poem, pick a tree near you and write your poem about it. When you complete your poem, turn it in to your teacher.

In Hardwood Groves
by: Robert Frost

The same leaves over and over again!
They fall from giving shade above
To Make one texture of faded brown
And fit the earth like a leather glove.

Before the leaves can mount again
To fill the trees with another shade,
They must go down past things coming up,
They must go down into the dark decayed.

They Must be pierced by flowers and put
Beneath the feet of dancing flowers.
However it is in some other world
I know that this is the way in ours.

TASK III
• You will now compose a poem that will describe the feelings (emotions) you felt as you observed the environment on a hike. Describe how seeing an animal or birds playing affected you, or describe the feeling of being alone with all of nature surrounding you. This poem will reflect your imagination as well as your feelings.

Suggestions for Writing Poetry

1. Use all the descriptive words you can think of to describe an object or emotion.

2. After you have written a poem, read it to yourself out loud and make corrections; delete or add words; shorten or lengthen phrases and sentences. Do this several times until you are really happy with your poem and yourself.

3. Always write what you feel. Don't be worried about what someone else might feel about how your poem describes something. A poem is for your satisfaction and not for someone else.

4. If you are going to have a title for a poem (this is not necessary) do this last. The title should come only after your poem is completed and edited by you.

Teaching Notes:

Group Poem I

Contributed By: Mitchell Sakofs, Outward Bound Inc.

Grade Level
All grades

Subject
Language Arts

Duration
One to two class periods

Objective
To provide students with an experience of creating a poem.

Materials
Poster paper (newsprint), masking tape, magic markers, and dictionaries.

Procedures
Circle up and introduce poetry. Read a poem or two that you have pre-selected for the group. They should be powerful, of interest to the students, and representative of different styles.

After a brief discussion about the poems, introduce the following group poem-writing exercise by identifying a topic that they will write about. The topic can be anything, but to start, it should be something the students have feelings about.

Go around the group, solicit from each a word or short phrase that captures various qualities about the topic, e.g., emotions associated with it, physical descriptions of it, intuitive connections between the topic and the individual.

Write these phrases on the newsprint then divide the class into small groups and give them about 10 minutes to create a poem using the words that were generated. (They are allowed to add short phrases, conjunctions or whatever, in order to weave the pieces into a whole.)

Have the groups read their poems to the class and leave time for discussion.

Group Poem II

Contributed By: Mitchell Sakofs, Outward Bound, Inc.

Grade Level
• All grades

Subject
• Language Arts

Duration
• One to two class periods

Objective
• To gain an understanding of and use imagery in creating a poem.

Procedures
• Circle up and have people reflect on how they are feeling about the physical space they are in.

• Introduce the idea of writing a group poem, and for that process identify an individual to serve as "The Master Poet," and a small group of two or three individuals to serve as "Composers." The rest will serve as "Sensors."

• The Master Poet's role is to physically place individuals functioning as Sensors to observe something. This "something" can be a scene, an object, or whatever. The Sensors generate words based their on assigned abilities, such as, seeing, hearing, smelling, touching, emotion, et cetera. The words generated by the Sensors are recorded by the composers who, in turn, use these raw materials to create a group poem.

• Encourage the Master Poet to be creative in locating Sensors. So for example, if the group is writing about trees, they may choose to place Sensors with eyes closed and arms wrapped around the tree; with eyes closed caressing the bark; eyes open, nose to the tree trunk. People could also be positioned to look at shadows, listening to wind moving the leaves, and so on.

• This kind of writing can be an effective way to consider the emotions, thoughts and feelings associated with another activity, either before, during or after the activity itself.

Teaching Notes:

Group Story and Write

Contributed By: Flo Levin, North Carolina Outward Bound School

Grade Level
• All grades

Subject
• Language Arts

Duration
• One class period

Objective
• To have students become excited about writing, observe the writing process, and draw upon their own knowledge of writing to contribute to a jointly authored story.

Materials
• Poster paper (newsprint), masking tape, magic markers, and dictionaries.

Procedures
Circle up. The teacher introduces the idea of a group writing exercise and then working off a pre-chosen theme—ideally one that

generates rich images in the students' minds — the instructor calls for phrases, sentences and thoughts.

Carefully selecting ideas, the instructor painstakingly models correct writing by asking the students specific questions about form, structure and content. (Example: "O.K., I'm starting the sentence, how should it look? How do you spell that?

What punctuation mark is needed here?") As the sentence is developed, the instructor puts it on the poster paper.

With careful questioning and group facilitation, the instructor engages the entire class in crafting a story. In the end, the group has a completed piece that they collaborated on and are proud of.

Extension
Exciting interactive conversation can be generated after a profound experience. Adventurous activities such as rock climbing, rappelling or service are good starting points for this excercise.

Unit IV

153

Teaching Notes:

Creative Writing in a Foreign Language

Contributed By:
George P. Armstrong,
Thompson Island Outward Bound Center

Grade Level
• High School

Subject
• Foreign language

Duration
• Three to five class periods

Objectives
During this activity the student will:

• Translate a list of words common to the things found in nature;

• Learn the components of getting started in creative writing;

• Write a short story about an experience on a field trip and increase their working vocabulary in the foreign language (s)he is studying.

Procedures

TASK 1 — Translation
• Student Assignment - Translate the list of vocabulary words on this page.

• Activity Test - The teacher will use an overhead projector to flash the list of vocabulary words on a screen. The student must translate each word.

VOCABULARY LIST

Mushroom _____
Fir _____
Moss _____
Twig _____
Fox _____
Water _____
Beaver _____
Pond _____
Skunk _____
Meadow _____
Fish _____
Sky _____
Bird _____
Peaceful _____
Brush _____
Moist _____
Birch _____
Summer _____

Log _____
West _____
Cone _____
Nest _____
Marsh _____
Weed _____
Sun _____
Rabbit _____
Fresh _____
Chipmunk _____
Spring _____
Snake _____
North _____
Grasshopper _____
South _____
Willow _____
East _____
Tree _____
Wildflower _____
Branch _____
Grass _____
Seasons _____
Raccoon _____
Stream _____
Squirrel _____
Forest _____
Deer _____
Wind _____
Spider _____
Beautiful _____
Frog _____
Clear _____
Duck _____
Rocky _____
Bush _____
Fall _____
Sand _____
Winter _____

TASK 2 — Getting Started
Writing is communication. What we must learn is how to communicate in a systematic way on paper so that our thoughts come out clearly and are understandable by the reader. The following are some points we should think about, and maybe make little notes on, before we start writing:

• Select a subject that is meaningful to you, both intellectually as well as emotionally.

• Write about something that you feel good about, i.e., an event, a person, a place, an experience, etc.

• Sit and think about your topic for a while before you start.

• When thinking about your topic you may want to formulate a variety of searching questions such as: Why? What? How? When? Where? It is sometimes helpful to write the answers to these questions on 3" x 5" cards for future reference to help in your recall.

Teaching Notes:

- You should organize your ideas first. How are you going to start off? What are you going to say in the middle? How are you going to close?

- After you have completed these four steps you are ready to begin. Instead of writing one draft, write three quick drafts. Don't ponder one particular draft, but write from materials and thoughts you gather from the first five steps. When you have completed the three drafts, reread each draft. It is recommended that you read each draft out loud. The ear will catch what you missed with your eye. Look for these three: sentence structure, repetition, and wording. Then pick your best draft and build from there. Remember, don't get discouraged if you have to do this many times before it comes out right. At times veteran writers rewrite their materials as many as 15-20 times.

TASK 3 — **Writing Assignments**
Student assignment — Go walking or sit in a wooded area, marsh, lake shore or in a field. Observe what you are seeing and feeling, listen for sounds, take a couple of deep breaths, touch the objects around you. You should record some of your thoughts while doing this.

Once you have gathered the information (food for thought), return to the classroom and start writing a short story about your experience in the language you are studying, using as many words as possible from your vocabulary list.

Unit IV

Into The Classroom:

Teaching Notes:

SHAKESPEARE

Contributed By:
George P. Armstrong,
Thompson Island Outward
Bound Center

Grade Level
• High School

Subject
• Literature

Duration
• Three to five class periods

Objectives
As part of this activity, you will read selections of Shakespeare which refer to plants, identify these plants in local natural settings and through this experience come to a better understanding of metaphor, symbolism, and the overall effect that Shakespeare conveys through his references to nature.

Activities
The student is required to complete all of the following exercises and do the following for each exercise:

• Read the selection first.

• Note each reference to a plant in the selection.

• Read the additional assignments (from which the first selection was extracted) in order to understand the context in which the selection appears.

• Using the plant descriptions, find the plant in its natural seting, taking time to observe it.

• Answer the questions that go along with each selec-

tion and follow any other instructions. The answers should be long enough to answer the question completely. Remember, your understanding of the subject will be reflected in your answers. Take time to answer completely.

Selections
• (*Titus Andronicus II. IV." "*)
"O, had the monster seen those lily hands Tremble, like aspen-leaves upon a lute."

Read entire *Act II* of *Titus Andronicus* then answer these questions.

• Why has Shakespeare chosen the lily in his description?

• Why has he chosen the aspen as opposed to another type of tree?

• After reviewing these plants, what was the effect, if any, on your understanding of the passage?

156

Teaching Notes:

• (*Othello IV. iii 41.*)
The poor soul sat sighing by a sycamore tree,
Sing all a green willow;
Her hand on her bosom her head on her knee,
Sing, willow, willow, willow;
The fresh streams ran by her, and murmur's her moans;
Sing willow, willow, willow;
Her salt tears fell from her, and softened the stones;
Lay be these;
Sing willow, willow, willow;
Prithee, hie thee; he'll come anon:
Sing all a green willow must be my garland.
Let nobody blame him; his scorn I approve,
Nay, that's not next. Hark! who isn't that knocks?
Emil. It's the wind.
I call'd my love false love; but what said he then?
Sing willow, willow, willow;
If I court mow women, you'll couch mow men.

Read *Act IV of Othello*, paying careful attention to the relationship of the selection above to the entire act, then answer these questions.

• What emotion is conveyed through this passage?

• What are the characteristics of a willow tree that Shakespeare has used to convey this particular emotion in the passage?

• (*The Merry Wives of Windsor IV. iv. 28*)
"There is an old tale goes that Herne the hunter,
Sometime a keeper here in Windsor forest,
Doth all the winter-time, at still midnight,
Walk round about an oak, with great ragg'd horns;
Why yet there want not many that do fear
n deep of night to walk by this Herne's oak.

Read *Act VI* from *the Merry Wives of Windsor*, then answer the following questions.

• What is the significance of "Herne's Oak" in these selections?

• Go out in a wooded area and pick out a tree that you feel could represent "Herne's Oak." Then write down your reasons for choosing the particular tree that you picked.

• (*The Comedy of Errors II. ii. 176*)
Thou are an elm, my husband, I a vine,
Whose weakness married to thy stronger state,
Makes me with thy strength to communicate:
If aught possess thee from me, it is dross,
Usurping ivy, briar, or idle moss;
Who, all for want of pruning, with intrusion
Infect thy sap, and live on thy sap, and live on thy confsion.

Read *Act II* of *the Comedy of Errors* and answer these questions.

• Is the use of plants here purely descriptive? If not, what is the function of the plants in the selection?

• How does the relationship between the characters mentioned in this selection (and the rest of the act) compare to the relationship between the tree and vine or moss as you have found them in the wilderness? Discuss in depth.

OPTIONAL ACTIVITIES

This section contains one optional activity which may be done for extra credit. This question will require some research in order to complete it thoroughly. Use the library.

Throughout Shakespeare's plays, there are constant references to flowers. In many of these instances, there is a special significance to the type of flower written about. Apart from

Unit IV

Teaching Notes:

their beauty and aroma, flowers were also used during Shakespeare's time as symbols or badges in the coats-of-arms of families. Certain flowers were also used by her balists during Shakespeare's time for their supposed medical properties. Of course flowers are also mentioned as an adornment.

Read: The following selections and then through your own research, answer the questions. You may have to look these selections up in the play inorder to better understand them.

1. "Cropped are the flower-de-luces in your arms; of England's coat one half is cast away," (Henry, VI. I. i. 80)
2. "The vagabond flag upon the stream" (Antony and Cleopatra, I. iv. 45)
3. "Now by my maiden honour, yet as pure As the unsullied lily;" (Love's Labour's Lost, V. ii. 351)
4. She must, the saints must have her; yet a virgin, A most unspotted lily shall she pass To the ground, and all the world shall mourn her. (Henry VIII., V. v. 60)

Questions

- The "flower-de-luces" in selection 1 are thought to be the iris flower, also known as a "flag." What is the significance of the flower in this passage? After observing an iris, in your opinion, why was this particular flower the prototype for the often used "flower-de-luce" in Shakespeare's plays?

- After observing the flag or iris in the woods, how does Shakespeare's description of this flower in selection 2 compare to the way and place where you found it growing in the woods?

- What is the lily a symbol for in selections 3 and 4?

Plant Identification Guide

WILLOW: tree, various heights according to species, long narrow alternate simple leaves, sometimes leaves droop as in the weeping willow. On other species dropping is not a noticeable. Has ridged bark.

ASPEN: Tree, fine tooth triangular shaped leaves, dark brown twigs, chalky looking bark.

OAK: Tree, very large when mature, simple alternate deeply lobed leaves, buds cluster at tip of twigs. Has ridged bark.

ELM: Tree, very large when mature, alternate simple leaves, double toothed, feather veined leaves, furrowed greyish bark.

LILY: Bulbed perennials with parallel veined leaves. Flowers usually bell-like or triangular. These flowers usually have 3 or 6 petals. Wild and cultivated.

IRIS: Plants with flat sword like or grass like leaves ranged edge to edge. Flower parts in groups of threes.

(Note: A tree and flower guide might be helpful in locating these plants.

Kurt Hahn

Selected Quotations:

It is wrong to coerce people into opinions, but it is a duty to impel them into experiences.

* * * * *

Persuasion, Compulsion and Attraction. You can preach at them: that is the hook without a worm; you can order them to volunteer: that is dishonest; you can call on them: you are needed: and that appeal hardly ever fails.

* * * * *

Your disability is your opportunity.

* * * * *

We need to be able to feel that as a people we are just and kindly. On this consciousness depends on our inner strength.

The scientific and technical progress which we have witnessed in our life time has been immense. But it has been accompanied by a deterioration human worth. Something indefinable has been lost. I can only hint at it.

* * * * *

I regard it as the foremost task of education to insure the survival of these qualities: an enterprising curiosity, an indefatigable spirit, tenacity in pursuit, readiness for sensible self-denial, and above all, compassion.
If you want me to open a school in this castle it must be for more than a Boarding school for well-to-do boys. Your Boarding school is only justified if it gives health to the district. I do not want the craftsmen to come into this Castle and teach in our atmosphere; I want you to send the boys to the craftsmen of the surrounding villages—the carpenter, the blacksmith, the wheelwright, the

wood-carver, the sculptor, the engineer and the locksmith. You will find that the good artisan has a greater horror of unfinished work than the schoolmaster. From the first, this school must be open to promising day children irrespective of the financial position of the parents. [Written by Hahn and attributed by him to Prince Max von Baden]

* * * * *

The decline of initiative as a result of the widespread disease of 'spectatoritis'; the decline of fitness as a result of modern means of locomotion; the decline of skill and care as a result of the weakening tradition of craftsmanship; the decline of concern about one's neighbor as a result of the unseemly haste with which the daily life is conducted.

* * * * *

I have often shown the Gordonstown (or Salem) Final Report from to teachers at Secondary Schools. These are the headlines: Esprit de Corps. Sense of Justice. Ability to state facts precisely. Ability to follow out what he believes to be the right course in the face of Discomforts, Hardships, Dangers, Mockery, Boredom, Skepticism, impulses of the moment. Ability to plan. Imagination. Ability to organize, shown in the disposition of work and in the direction of young boys. Ability to deal with the unexpected. Degree of mental concentration, where the task in question interests him, and where it does not. Conscientiousness, in everyday affairs, in tasks with which he is specially entrusted. Manners. Manual dexterity. Standard reached in school subjects. Practical Work. Art Work. Physical Exercises, fighting spirit, endurance, reaction time.
Every normal youth longs for occasions to prove himself, body and soul, with all he has in human strength. A

society which in peacetime denies satisfaction to this longing is asking for trouble: through unwittingly building up an emotional power—sinister and unpredictable and in permanent readiness—which is often unconsciously ready to welcome war as a release from frustration. The student of history will know of international crises during which this hidden power has burst forth, flooding the judgment of responsible men and women and weighting the scales in favor of war... "Outward Bound" will serve peace if it succeeds in enlisting the devotion of the young in the service of their fellow man "in danger and in need."

* * * * *

Whoever saves a life will never take a life.
May the great decision be taken to revise the unhealthy balance between passivity and action as it now prevails in the secondary school of Europe and America, sapping the human strength of our adolescents, and may this task be tackled without the fear of impeding our children in their academic progress. Is it too much to hope that future secondary schools, particularly those in big cities, will run "Outward Bound" homes in the country? To them would be sent regularly their boys and girls for a month's course during which only one subject would be taught, preferably one connected with the study of the surrounding world, its plant and animal life or its historical and architectural heritage.

* * * * *

In August 1945 I went to Berlin. I stayed with an American who will be remembered as one of the Good Samaritans of this period: he had run great risks to save people in Russian-occupied territory. He asked me to go to the Lehrter station where the German refugees were arriving in cattle trucks. We went in a car driven by a young American corporal, a kindly-looking man. We passed through scenes of misery and death which will haunt me all my life, and all the while the corporal's radio played jazz. Finally my Good Samaritan leant forward and said: "For God's sake, stop." The young man had a dispersed soul which he could not even assemble before the majesty of death.

* * * * *

Rescue service will have a place of honor in the timetable, uniting members of different nations through the common bond of active humanity.

* * * * *

Are you in earnest about the ideals which you proclaim? Who shall give an answer? Free young men and women trained to render hard and willing service, ready to do as the Good Samaritan has done.

* * * * *

This cheese goes straight to the soul.

* * * * *

We need opportunities for active service in peace-time.

Suggested Readings

Brereton, Henry L., Gordonstoun: Ancient Estate and Modern School (London: Ward R. Chambers, Ltd., 1968)

Cousins, Emily,, Melissa Rodgers eds., Fieldwork - An Expeditionary Learning Outward Bound Reader, (Kendall /Hunt Publishing Company, Dubuque, Iowa, 1995).

Crenshaw, Larry, The North Carolina Outward Bound Earthbook, Morganton, NC: The North Carolina Outward bound School, 1994.

Darling, John, "New Life and New Education: The Philosophies of Davidson, Reddie and Hahn," Scottish Education Review 13 (May 192): 12-24.

Day, John H., "The Basic Conception of Education of Kurt Hahn and Its Translation into Practice" (M.Ed. thesis, University of Queensland, 1980).

Darst, Paul W., George P. Armstrong, Outdoor Adventure Activities For School and Recreation Programs, Waveland Press, Inc., Prospect Heights, IL, 1980.

Duckworth, Eleanor, The Having of Wonderful Ideas and Other Essays on Teaching and Learning, Teachers College Press, 1987.

Fluegelman, Andrew, ed., The New Games Book, Dolphin Books/Dcubleday & Company, Inc., Garden City, NY, 1976.

Hahn, Kurt, "Outward Bound," Yearbook of Education 1957, 1957 pp. 436-462.

James, Thomas, "Kurt Hahn and the Aims of Education," Journal of Experiential Education 13 (May 1990): 6-13.

James, Thomas, "Sketch of Moving Spirit: Kurt Hahn," Journal of Experiential Education 3 (Spring 1980): 17-22.
Miner, Joshua L., Joe Boldt, Outward Bound USA, William Morrow and Company, Inc., New York, NY, 1981.

Richards, Anthony, "Kurt Hahn: The Midwife of Educational Ideas" (Ed.D. dissertation, University of Colorado at Boulder, 1981).

Rohnke, Karl, Cowstails and Cobras II - A Guide to Games, Initiatives, Ropes Courses, & Adventure Curriculum, Project Adventure, Inc., Hamilton, MA, and Kendall/Hunt Publishing Company, Dubuque, Iowa, 1989.

Rohnke, Karl, Project Adventure, Project Adventure, Inc., Hamilton, MA, 1974.

Rohnke, Karl, Silver Bullets, Project Adventure, Inc., Hamilton, MA, and Kendall/Hunt Publishing Company, Dubuque, Iowa, 1984.

Rohnke, Karl, Butler, Steve, QuickSilver, Kendall/Hunt Publishing Company, Dubuque, Iowa, 1995.

Rohrs, Herman, "The Realm of Education in the Thought of Kurt Hahn," Comparative Education Review 3 (November 1966): 21-32.

Rohrs, Herman, and H. Turnstall Behrens, eds., Kurt Hahn (London: Routledge & Kegan Paul, 1970).

Schoel, Jim, Dick Prouty, Paul Radcliffe, Islands of Healing - A Guide to Adventure Based Counseling, Project Adventure, Inc., Hamilton, MA, 1988.

Skidelsky, Robert, English Progressive Schools (London: Penguin Books, 1969).

Ylvisaker, Paul, "The Missing Dimension," speech made at the Third Outward Bound International Conference," Garrison: Outward Bound, Inc., 1988.

Outward Bound Resources

Colorado Outward Bound School
945 Pennsylvania Street
Denver, CO   80203-3198
1-800-477-2627 (phone)
1-303-831-6987 (fax)

Hurricane Island Outward Bound School
P. O. Box 429
Rockland, ME   04841
1-800-341-1744 (phone)
1-207-594-9425 (fax)

New York City Outward Bound Center
140 West Street, Suite 2626
New York, NY   10007
1-212-608-8899 (phone)
1-212-608-9250 (fax)

North Carolina Outward Bound School
121 North Sterling Street
Morganton, NC   28655-3443
1-800-841-0186 (phone)
1-704-437-0094 (fax)

Pacific Crest Outward Bound School
0110 S.W. Bancroft Street
Portland, OR   97201
1-800-547-3312 (phone)
1-503-274-7722 (fax)

Thompson Island Outward Bound
  Education Center
P. O. Box 127
Boston, MA   02127-0002
1-617-328-3900 (phone)
1-617-328-3710 (fax)

Voyageur Outward Bound School
111 Third Avenue South
Minneapolis, MN   55401-2551
1-800-328-2943 (phone)
1-612-338-3540 (fax)

Expeditionary Learning Outward Bound
122 Mount Auburn Street
Cambridge, MA   02138
1-617-576-1260 (phone)
1-617-576-1340 (fax)
info@elob.ci.net (e-mail)

Harvard Outward Bound Project in
  Experienced-Based Learning
Harvard Graduate School of Education
Gutman Library, 4th Floor
Cambridge, MA   02138
1-617-496-5220 (phone)
1-617-496-3095 (fax)

Outward Bound National Office
Route 9D, R2 Box 280
Garrison, NY   10524-9757
1-800-243-8520 (phone)
1-914-424-4280 (fax)

INDEX